RECAPITULATIONS

**STUDIES IN PHILOSOPHY
AND THE HISTORY OF PHILOSOPHY**

General Editor: Jude P. Dougherty

**Studies in Philosophy
and the History of Philosophy   Volume 26**

Recapitulations
Essays in Philosophy

by Thomas Prufer

THE CATHOLIC UNIVERSITY OF AMERICA PRESS
Washington, D.C.

Copyright © 1993
The Catholic University of America Press
All rights reserved
Printed in the United States of America

The paper in this publication meets the minimum requirements of
American National Standards for Information Science—
Permanence of Paper for Printed Library Materials,
ANSI Z39.48–1984.

∞

LIBRARY OF CONGRESS CATALOGING-IN-PUBLICATION DATA
Prufer, Thomas, 1929–
    Recapitulations : essays in philosophy / by Thomas Prufer.
      p. cm. — (Studies in philosophy and the history of
philosophy ; v. 26)
    Includes bibliographical references.
    ISBN 978–0–8132–3064–1 (pbk)
    1. Philosophy. I. Title. II. Series.
B21.S78 vol. 26
[B29]
100 s—dc20
[100]
                91-44978

This book is dedicated to Frank Slade.
What is best in it I owe to him.
In the fifty years I have known him,
I have learned from him what it is to be
friend, philosopher, Catholic.

I am also indebted to Robert Sokolowski,
friend and colleague. See Plato, *Protagoras*
348c7–d5.

I am grateful to Professor Gadamer for his
encouragement at crucial times during the
last twenty-five years, to Yves Simon and
Henry Deku for being models of the art of
teaching, to the memory of Elizabeth
Whitelaw, *sine qua non*, to Marianna's
"hidden face," to Jude Dougherty, Dean of
the School of Philosophy of The Catholic
University of America, and to my students.

I wish to thank Susan Needham, Mark
Hurley, Anne Theilgard, David McGonagle,
and Brevis Press for the production of the
book.

Contents

	Foreword	ix
	Preface	xi
	Chronology and Acknowledgments of Previous Publication	xv
1.	The Dramatic Form of Plato's *Phaedo*	1
2.	Aristotelian Themes	6
3.	Providence and Imitation: Sophocles' *Oedipus Rex* and Aristotle's *Poetics*	12
4.	Notes on Nature The City and the Garden Nature and Gods in Epicureanism Hobbes's Sovereign Teaching	22
5.	A Reading of Augustine's *Confessions*, Book X	27
6.	Creation, Solitude and Publicity	32
7.	Juxtapositions: Aristotle, Aquinas, Strauss	35
8.	A Reading of Hume's *A Treatise of Human Nature*	43
9.	Husserlian Distinctions and Strategies in *The Crisis*	48
10.	Quotation and Writing, Egos and Tokenings, Variables and Gaps	58
11.	The Logic of Modernity	66
12.	Husserl, Heidegger, Early and Late, and Aquinas	72
13.	The Death of Charm and the Advent of Grace: Waugh's *Brideshead Revisited*	91
	Scholium I (Chapter 11): Two Doxologies: Argument and Praise	103
	Scholium II (Chapter 12): Glosses on Heidegger's Architectonic Word-Play	105
	Scholium III (Chapter 12): Heidegger between (Gadamer's) Plato and Aristotle	110

Foreword

All of these essays except the first part of Chapter 4 and Scholia I and III have been previously published.

The first two paragraphs of the original of Chapter 2 have been omitted. The first three paragraphs of that essay in its present form have been revised and expanded. The fourth paragraph is new.

Part of Chapter 5 was published in a somewhat different form as part of "A Protreptic: What Is Philosophy?" (1963). Some additions to the text as published in 1982 have been made in the footnotes.

The text of Chapter 6 as published in 1986 was marred by unauthorized revision. The errors have been corrected and the text has been slightly emended.

In Chapter 9 the line references to *Husserliana* are added.

Chapter 10 is the second of three parts of the essay published in *Philosophische Rundschau* in 1974.

Chapter 13 has two additions.

There are some other additions and excisions, precisions and revisions.

The occasion of writing marks the style of some of these essays. Chapter 2 was written as an encyclopedia article, Chapter 11 as a book review, Chapter 12 as a lecture.

In general the style is like that characterized by ancient rhetoricians as the *abruptum sermonis genus*. Aquinas's *modus loquendi formalissimus* and the *catenae aureae* of Deku's lectures and essays were models.

"Lucidity does not imply universal intelligibility. . . . The test of lucidity is whether a statement can be read as meaning anything other than what it intends."[1]

I have not always followed Fowler and Follet on the use of "that" and "which."

References given without quoting the text referred to will be useful to those who care to look them up, but the texts referred to are not

---

1. Evelyn Waugh, "Literary Style in England and America," in *The Essays, Articles and Reviews of Evelyn Waugh*, ed. Donat Gallagher (London: Methuen, 1983), p. 478.

essential to the exposition. Untranslated texts are important but not essential to the exposition.

In Chapter 4 the note on Hobbes seems out of place, but it is a foil for formulating the specificity of Epicureanism: the similarities between Hobbes and Epicureanism highlight their differences; and Epicureanism, in spite of (or because of) its differences from Plato and Aristotle, cannot be left out of an attempt to formulate the specificity of "the ancients" in their differences from "the moderns."

Aristotle serves as a foil to Plato, Epicurus and Lucretius, Aquinas, Hobbes, Hume, and Nietzsche. Husserl serves as a foil to Heidegger.

The book is a whole, not a mere collection, not what Aristotle calls "a heap" (*sōros*; see Chapter 3), but a unified and organic work: the parts are not merely juxtaposed but affect and comment on one another.

Preface

"I mean 'three white leopards sat under a juniper tree,'" T. S. Eliot is said to have said in answer to the question "What do you mean by 'three white leopards sat under a juniper tree'?"[1] Translation, paraphrase, and summary are always betrayals.

In a way there is no way to say what this book is "about" except by resaying the book itself. Choice of one word rather than another, sequence, anticipation and recapitulation, cross-reference and self-quotation, allusion—all these are generative of meaning and they are lost in paraphrase or summary.

Dante[2] makes a distinction between *forma tractandi* and *forma tractatūs*. The inseparability of "what is spoken about" and "how it is spoken about" is not only a characteristic of the book itself (if the catachresis[3] "a book speaks" be permitted), a characteristic of the style (*in actu exercito*) of the book; it is also one of the themes (*in actu signato*) of the book. This is most obvious in the analyses of Plato's *Phaedo*, Sophocles' *Oedipus Rex*, Augustine's *Confessions*, and Waugh's *Brideshead Revisited*. But it is also obvious, on the "micrological" level, in the frequent use of Greek, Latin, and German words.

This points to another theme: how are nonphilosophical uses of language troped or twisted into philosophical uses? This question is raised in terms of the question, What is the relation between the nominative form of the dative of manifestation, Husserl's transcendental ego in the *epochē*, and "I" in the sense involved with "the mouth that speaks the word 'I'" (Frege), a word in the language I am speaking (leaving aside the issue of the homonyms "eye" and "aye")? This question is approached in terms of the grafting or imbrication of sign systems and in terms of different kinds of quotation.

Open-endedness and closure in philosophical uses of language in Plato and an analysis of tropings in the later Heidegger begin and end the treatment of this theme.

1. *Ash Wednesday* II.
2. Letter to Can Grande.
3. Cf. "the arms of a chair; the legs of a table."

The book tells two stories, two among others. Both stories are stories about shifts, shifts that show themselves as shifts by preserving what they shift from. (The new is inscribed over the old; the old is legible beneath the new: palimpsest.) The first story is the story of shifts in senses of the word "nature." The second story is the story of shifts in senses of the word "being" in Aquinas and in Heidegger.

"Nature" is a term of contrast. The discovery of the primacy of nature brings with it a depreciation of the artificial and the conventional. But nature shows a prodigious power of ingesting what it is contrasted with, its "other." The nature of the artificial and the nature of the conventional become themes. The question "What?" or "What kind?"[4] is asked of the artificial and the conventional. This is one way of formulating "the Socratic turn," a turn which led to characterizing the beginning of philosophy anachronistically as "pre-Socratic." (The articulation of being into the natural, on the one hand, and the artificial and the conventional, on the other hand, would seem to be one way of exhausting the senses of "being.")

Reverberations in philosophy of the theme of creation *ex liberalitate* and *ex nihilo* led to an identification of the freedom to choose between alternatives (being alone and not being alone) with divine self-sufficiency and necessity, with divine nature. This identification reached its acme in Aquinas.

The rejection of this identity, the splitting of freedom off from nature, the claim that freedom lords it over nature, sets the stage for a depreciation of nature(s) to mere material to be mastered and to an obstacle to creativity, an obstacle to be overcome by power freed from nature(s). But as the philosophical poet says, "You can throw nature out with a pitchfork, but it will come back, breaking in unexpectedly, victorious over your perverse contempt."[5]

Aquinas and Heidegger are two turning points in the history of the senses of "being." The foil for both Aquinas and Heidegger is Aristotle's doctrine of *ousia* as *eidos* and as *noēsis noēseōs* without production and action and without friendship.

Aquinas makes a distinction between *ens qua ens* as "the subject (matter) of metaphysics" and *ens primum et necessarium* as "the principle of the subject (matter) of metaphysics." Preserving this distinction, Aquinas nevertheless makes a shift to *esse commune* (*completum et simplex sed non subsistens*),[6] which falls within "the subject (matter) of meta-

---

4. Chaucer says "Dame Kind" for "Mother Nature." The German for "child" is "*Kind*"; cf. the English "kin" and "natal," "native," "nativity."

5. Horace, *Ep.* I, x, 24–25.

6. *De potentia Dei* I, 1. I learned the importance of this formula from Ferdinand Ulrich.

physics" although not identical with *ens qua ens* or *ens commune*, and to *esse irreceptum subsistens*, "the principle of the subject (matter) of metaphysics."⁷

Heidegger makes a distinction between that-which-*is*-(present/absent) or (manifest/hidden) and presencing/absencing or manifesting/hiding. The interplay of presencing/absencing as *Entbergung/Verbergung* (*alētheia/lēthē*) is for Heidegger *Sein* as such (or *Seyn*, not *Sein des Seienden*), which was not thematized by what Heidegger calls "metaphysics." Preserving this distinction, Heidegger nevertheless makes a shift to the proper space (*Ereignis, Lichtung*) of protectedness (*Bergung*) beyond the interplay of presencing/absencing, a shift to truth (*Wahrheit*) as protectedness (*Wahrnis*).

These two stories, the story about "nature" and the story about "being," have a subplot in common: the question whether these three pairs, part/whole, contingency/necessity, clarity/obscurity, are *anhypotheta*.⁸ Plato, Aquinas, and Heidegger go beyond these pairs, each in his own way: Plato beyond part/whole (*symplokē eidōn*)⁹ toward the One and the Indeterminate Two, Aquinas beyond contingency/necessity toward *esse irreceptum subsistens*, Heidegger beyond clarity/obscurity toward *Bergung* (and *Ereignis, Lichtung, Wahrnis*).

This preface is both too long and too short.¹⁰ Thinking of Hegel and remembering Eliot ("What we call the beginning is often the end / And to make an end is to make a beginning"),¹¹ perhaps we should say that the preface will make sense only when being reread after the book to which it is prefaced has been read.

---

7. John Wippel, "Thomas Aquinas and Participation," in *Studies in Medieval Philosophy*, ed. Wippel, Studies in Philosophy and the History of Philosophy, vol. 17 (Washington, D.C.: The Catholic University of America Press, 1987), pp. 117–58; Etienne Gilson, "L'Etre et Dieu," *Constantes philosophiques de l'être* (Paris: Vrin, 1983), pp. 169–230; cf. *Revue Thomiste* 62 (1962), 181–202, 398–416, esp. 398–406.

8. Plato, *Republic* 510b7, 511b6; Aristotle, *Metaphysics* 1005b14. Compare Robert Sokolowski, "Thinking Beyond Philosophy," in *Presence and Absence* (Bloomington: Indiana University Press, 1978), pp. 172–81.

9. The many *eidē* are interwoven with one another through similarity and difference (sameness and otherness) into one living whole (*zōon*). See Scholium III.

10. See the summaries of Chapters 4, 5, 6, and 11 and the three scholia.

11. Hegel, "Vorrede," *Die Phänomenologie des Geistes*; Eliot, *Little Gidding* V.

Chronology and Acknowledgments of Previous Publication

An earlier version of Chapter 5 was published as "A Protreptic: What is Philosophy?" in Studies in Philosophy and the History of Philosophy, Volume 2, edited by John K. Ryan, pp. 1–19 (Washington, D.C.: The Catholic University of America Press, 1963). A more recent version appeared as "Notes for a Reading of Augustine, *Confessions*, Book X" in *Interpretation* 10, Number 2/3 (May/September 1982), 197–200.

Part of Chapter 8 was published as "Notes on Interpreting Hume" in Studies in Philosophy and the History of Philosophy, Volume 4 (1969), edited by John K. Ryan, pp. 67–74.

Chapter 2, "Aristotelian Themes," appeared in Studies in Philosophy and the History of Philosophy, Volume 5 (1970), edited by John K. Ryan, pp. 73–78.

Chapter 10 was published as "Welt, Ich und Zeit in der Sprache" in *Philosophische Rundschau* 20, Number 3/4 (1974), 224–40.

Chapter 9 was published as "An Outline of Some Husserlian Distinctions and Strategies, Especially in *The Crisis*" in *Phänomenologische Forschungen*, Volume 1, edited by E. W. Orth (Freiburg und München: Verlag Karl Alber, 1975), pp. 89–104.

Chapter 8, "A Reading of Hume's *A Treatise of Human Nature*," was published in *The Review of Metaphysics* 30, Number 1 (September 1976), 115–19.

Chapter 13, "The Death of Charm and the Advent of Grace: Waugh's *Brideshead Revisited*," was published in *Communio* 10, Number 3 (Fall 1983), 281–91.

Chapter 6, "Creation, Solitude and Publicity," is reprinted from *Essays in Phenomenological Theology*, edited by Steven W. Laycock and James G. Hart, pp. 63–65 (Albany: State University of New York Press, 1986), by permission of the State University of New York Press.

Chapter 11, "The Logic of Modernity," was first published in *The Thomist* 50, Number 1 (January 1986), 151–57.

Chapter 1 was published as "The Dramatic Form of *Phaedo*" in *The Review of Metaphysics* 39, Number 3 (March 1986), 547–51.

Part of Chapter 4 was published as "Two Notes on Nature: Nature and Gods in Epicureanism; Hobbes's Sovereign Teaching" in the *Graduate Faculty Philosophy Journal* 11, Number 2 (1986), 107–10.

Chapter 12 was published as "Heidegger, Early and Late, and Aquinas" in *Edmund Husserl and the Phenomenological Tradition: Essays in Phenomenology*, edited by Robert Sokolowski, Volume 18 of Studies in Philosophy and the History of Philosophy (1988), pp. 197–215.

Chapter 3 was published as "Providence and Imitation: Sophocles's *Oedipus* and Aristotle's *Poetics*" in *Philosophy and Art*, edited by Daniel O. Dahlstrom, Volume 23 of Studies in Philosophy and the History of Philosophy (1991), pp. 1–10.

Scholium II appeared as "Glosses on Heidegger's Architectonic Word-Play: *Lichtung* and *Ereignis*, *Bergung* and *Wahrnis*" in *The Review of Metaphysics* 44, Number 3 (March 1991), 607–12.

Chapter 7, "Juxtapositions: Aristotle, Aquinas, Strauss," is from *Leo Strauss's Thought: Toward a Critical Engagement*, edited by Alan Udoff, pp. 115–21. Copyright © 1991 by Lynne Rienner Publishers, Inc. Reprinted by permission of the Publisher.

Scholium III, "Heidegger between (Gadamer's) Plato and Aristotle," will be published in *The Philosophy of Hans-Georg Gadamer* in The Library of Living Philosophers.

1

The Dramatic Form of Plato's *Phaedo*

That the itself-by-itself (*auto kath' hauto*, 100b4–7) is mediated to soul by (true) *logos* is itself mirrored by the dramatic form of *Phaedo*, the recollection of the last day of Socrates by Phaedo, who was himself there, to Echecrates, who was not there but who would gladly hear what Socrates said and how he died.

This thesis can be formulated in terms of relationships among the following:

(1) the dramatic form of *Phaedo*, that is, the mediating difference between the framework or the narration and what is framed and narrated;

(2) a cluster of four themes having to do with *logos*: (a) the flight to *logoi* as second sailing (99c9–d1, e5–6), that is, taking the oars in hand when the wind in the sails dies down (cf. the Odyssean raft which carries us *faute de mieux*, lacking a divine *logos*, 85d1); (b) "listen not to *me* but to (true) *logos*" (see 91c1–3); (c) "mourn not *my* death, but the death of the *logos* (by the kind of refutation that shows up falsity)" (see 89b9–10, c1); (d) mistrust of misology, trust in *logos*, that is, as far as *logos* goes, confidence in a triumph of life over death;

(3) the difference between the straight-forward way, that is, the first, simple-minded, crude, ignorant answer (100d4, 8), and the roundabout way, that is, the second, elegant, refined, clever answer (105c1–2), the answer which introduces mediation of the higher by the lower.

It is important that *Phaedo* is called *Phaedo* and not, in likeness to *The Defense of Socrates, The Last Day of Socrates*, and not, in likeness to *Euthyphro* or *Crito, Cebes and Simmias*. In form, *Phaedo* is what Phaedo says to Echecrates and what Echecrates says to Phaedo (neither are Athenians). Echecrates speaks about fifty lines; Phaedo speaks something more than two and one-half thousand lines. Phaedo quotes, in memorial repetition, what Socrates and his companions in speech said to one another, and he also describes what was done and suffered. We tend to forget the Chinese box or Russian doll structure of *Phaedo*:

2   RECAPITULATIONS

(Plato (Plato and Echecrates (Socrates and Cebes and Simmias))). We find ourselves listening not to what (Plato said) Phaedo says that Socrates or Cebes or Simmias said, but rather to what Socrates or Cebes or Simmias say. We lose ourselves in the speakers and their speeches presented in recollection and forget the recollecting speaker himself and his recollecting speech. But twice (88c8, 102a3) we are called back to the recollecting speech itself, to the framework (57a–59c) of presentation, by one who had been present, to one who was then absent, like Plato himself (although Phaedo is not sure, 59b10), absent from the last day of Socrates, absent from Socrates talking with his companions. Twice we are led to recollect that we are hearing Phaedo's speech recollecting to Echecrates what Socrates and his companions said to one another when Socrates was still Socrates and not yet a dead body and whatever else there may still be of Socrates besides his dead body. The unusualness of the "form" of these two returns (88c8, 102a3) to the framework (57a–59c) of presentation suggests that we give special weight and attention to their "content."

Sufficiency is lacking (see 70d4–5, 77d5–7, 84c5–7, 85b10–e2, 87e6, 92d2–5, 106d1, 6, 107a9–b9) in what had been said about whatever else there may still be of Socrates besides his dead body, except insofar as Phaedo's recollected words of Socrates and of his companions (insofar as Phaedo recollects accurately and completely; cf. 102a10, 103a4–5) are still words of Socrates and of his companions. The most important question which the dramatic form of *Phaedo* leads us to ask, without *Phaedo* answering that question sufficiently, is this: How are Socrates' *logoi* still *logoi* of Socrates and nevertheless able to be presented to Echecrates (and to us) by (Plato's) Phaedo's recollection of them after the death of Socrates? What is the relationship between Socrates' *logoi*, as spoken in repetition by Phaedo, and Socrates himself who first spoke them? What is one duality which is the unity of one and of another one (see 96e–97a; cf. 60b8–c1, 101b9ff.)? What is the one duality of Socrates and Phaedo in the one duality of what Socrates said and what Phaedo says he said? In whatever other way Socrates' soul may be deathless (Socrates himself is not deathless), the dramatic form of *Phaedo* shows us that insofar as *logoi* occupied Socrates himself (not merely his body and not his soul alone) and brought up whatever makes them, the *logoi*, able to be recollected as still one and the same after his death and also able to be recollected as not having been killed by the assaults of attempted refutations, so far does something of Socrates himself survive in a special way his becoming a dead body.

The difference between the first, simple-minded, crude, ignorant answer and the second, elegant, refined, clever answer is the difference between unmediated and mediated presence, and this difference is similar to the difference between being present oneself during the last day of Socrates and being told by another in recollection about the last day of Socrates. As hotness is to fire is to body heated by fire, so the itself-by-itself (*auto kath' hauto*, 100b4–7) is to (true) *logos* is to soul informed by (true) *logos*: *logos* is like mediating fire. As fire occupies body and brings up hotness, so (true) *logos* occupies soul and brings up the itself-by-itself. As fire mediates hotness to body, or as soul mediates life to body, so (true) *logos* mediates the itself-by-itself to soul. And so (Plato's) Phaedo mediates the *logoi* of Socrates' last day to Echecrates (and to us). As Theseus needed Ariadne, and Hercules needed Iolaus, so Socrates needs Phaedo.

Insofar as something itself-by-itself is deathless because it is not composed and therefore cannot be divided, and insofar as it is brought up or mediated to soul occupied by composed and divided *logoi* which have survived the assaults of attempted refutations, so far is soul itself deathless. It is not clear, certainly not sufficiently clear, how the itself-by-itself indwells *logos* and how *logos* indwells soul; but the dramatic form of *Phaedo* makes clear, first, that *logoi* can, in recollection, survive the one, both soul and body, whose they were, and in some way still are, although that one no longer is, and, second, that showing deathlessness by way of the irrefutability of *logoi* depends on their standing firm against assaults made in discussion, which in turn depends on being together with companions and not being only a soul or soul alone and merely a dead body.

Phaedo's mediating recollection of the last day of Socrates' talk with his companions tells us that the anticipation of death is an anticipation of deathlessness insofar as death is separation from what is composed and therefore can be divided (death as separation from the separable), and it shows us that the way to the deathlessness of the itself-by-itself (the uncomposed and therefore the indivisible) is by way of a second sailing, like Socrates' earlier flight from gazing on "the things" (99e3) and "the beings" (99e6) by themselves, that is, by way of a flight to *logoi*, which are in many ways composed and divided: for instance, *logoi* composed with and divided from the speakers whose they are (see 91c1–3); *logoi* composed with others by being agreed to by others (see esp. 89c3–11, 102a2) and divided from others by being disagreed with by others; *logoi* composed with or divided from, as true or false, what they are about; and each *logos* either composed with or divided from itself as well as either composed with or divided from other *logoi*.

Testing arguments together with companions by way of their counterarguments, which attack or try to drive away those arguments, clarifies somewhat the obscure kinship of soul with the itself-by-itself. Socrates prefers the deathlessness anticipated in formulating arguments (about deathlessness itself and about deathlessness of soul and about deathlessness of his soul; see 70c1–2, 107a1) and in refuting them, or in refuting attempts to refute them, to the quick death of a body not agitated by talking (63d5–e5). If the body is a prison, why not break jail by suicide? If besouling a body is a sickness of soul, why not sing a last song, shatter the lyre, administer the purging medicine to oneself and withdraw to the health of being a soul alone, a soul stripped of its cloak? Because the way up is by way of the way down, by way of the hard work of the second sailing, taking the oars in hand: the flight from blinding immediacy downward to mirroring *logoi*; the second, elegant, refined, clever answer: the defense of mediation.

Can there be immortal sayings of a mortal man? Perhaps, insofar as they are remembered to have been said in an immortal ("irrefutable") way about what is immortal ("the itself-by-itself "). Socrates and his companions are presented within a triangle whose three apexes are the itself-by-itself, soul, and *logoi*. But it is hard to grasp the three bonds (see 99c5–6) between these three: the bond between the itself-by-itself and soul, the bond between soul and *logos,* and the bond between *logos* and the itself-by-itself.

Just before Socrates is recollected by Phaedo to Echecrates to have spoken in the eschatological myth about being without a body as a highly and clearly bodily way of being, Socrates is recollected to have said that what had been said that day about the itself-by-itself and soul is insufficient.[1] A memorable day, but we are reminded how necessary it is to recall earlier days of Socrates, recounted, in other, later dialogues of Plato. We wonder how soul is both soul as cognate with whatever it knows and soul as enlivening of whatever body it besouls.

---

1. Does the last argument prove either too little (whatever is living is alive so long as it is alive, that is, not-dead; cf. 103e5) or too much (even noncognitive souls cannot perish; they will never cease to be, because they necessarily bear the form Life) or, the extremes touching, both? See "objections to the principle of exclusion of opposites" among the criticisms by Strato as translated by Hackforth in his commentary on *Phaedo*.

Socrates goes from "deathless" to "imperishable" without sufficient argument. Only Forms are eternal; human soul as cognitive, turned toward Forms in eros, participates in this eternity through the mediation of *logoi* that are irrefutable insofar as they participate in Forms. See 106d1 and 107b2.

Why live a Socratic life of philosophical *meletē* if *every* soul merely as soul (70d7–9, 94a8–9) is deathless and imperishable? Love of (true) *logoi* is a way to assimilate cognitive soul as cognitive to that which is imperishable. "Philosophical life" takes on a precise sense through the representation of the last day of Socrates in the dramatic form of *Phaedo*. Whether *that* life perishes or not depends on how well we remember and how well we refute.

We wonder how the composition-and-division of *logos* with itself and with other *logoi* affects its mediation of the itself-by-itself which it brings up to the souls it occupies. And we also wonder, in a special way, first whether and then how itself-by-itselfs are composed with and divided from one another (cf. *Sophist* 259e4–6).

We wonder whether or not the departed bee has after all left its sting behind (91c5; see 63c8–d2). Such a sting could be the gift of a way to a kind of deathlessness.[2]

2. Additional references: 57a1 (*autos*), a4 (*autos*); 58c8–9 (*pareinai*); 59a3–4, c7; 61b4–5; 63c8–d2; 64c1–2; 70b6–7; 72e3–4; 75d2–3; 76b8–9, e4–5, e9; 77a9; 77c10–78d7; 84c1–d3; 85b10–d10; 86d8, e1, e4; 88c1–8, d1–3, d7–9; 89a1–7, b9–c4, d1–3; 90b4–91c5, c8–e2; 91c11–92e3; 92d9–e3; 95a1–2, b1–3, e2–5; 100a1–3, b1–3, d5–6 (*parousia*); 101c9–102a1; 102a6–9, c1–8 (cf. 91c1–3); 103a4–6; 105b5–c8; 107a8–b9; 108d8–9; 110b1; 114d1–2; 115c7–8; 116a4–5. This essay was completed before I read Ronna Burger's excellent *The PHAEDO: A Platonic Labyrinth* (New Haven and London: Yale University Press, 1984); after reading her book, I have not found it necessary to change anything in my essay, except to indicate the similarity between 59b10 and 102a10.

2
Aristotelian Themes

We do not know our way about in the most radical question, "What is being?" a theme of endless inquiry. Justification of answers to this question is the science being sought; found, this science would be first philosophy, free because not subordinate, and, having the fewest principles, exact, or theology, the science of what is called divine because it is most excellent. Answers to the question will be complex: being is said in many irreducibly different senses, but being is also said with reference to one ruling or primary sense. Biological and astronomical processes, on the one hand, and the achievements of speech and art and virtue, on the other hand, are the context within which answers to the question are sought. Because what it means to be a being is not separable from beings, the term *ousia* (beingness) is accurately translated "entity" (not "substance"). The one word "entity" expresses the unity in the irreducible polarity between the foreground "*a* being" and the background "what leads us to call a being being: being*ness*." (Usually we use two words; for example, "a human" and "humanness.") Being or entity as a theme of inquiry is perplexing. What are the resources of this unusual inquiry?

In his inquiries Aristotle is concerned to leave undisturbed or to restore what is at first and usually manifest and said. Entity is not only what is said of something; it is also that of which something is said but which itself is not said of anything. Entity is not only being able to see but also seeing, and entity as activity is more primarily that activity which is not subordinate to a result and which is not over with because it is complete. (Housebuilding is for the sake of the house being built; healing ceases when health is achieved.) Entity is form, always itself, one and the same; for example, what it means to be sphere (neither "a sphere" nor "sphereness"); being in this sense is manifest against a background (192b34) of process but itself neither comes to be nor ceases to be. Entity is also that which comes to be and ceases to be; this lump of bronze is forged into a brazen sphere, and this brazen sphere is melted down into a lump of bronze. Entity is use or importance; being an axe is not so much being of iron or being in o shape as being for cutting. A shoe is for wearing and a house is for sheltering. Structure is subordinate to function and picturing to narrating. A stone flute and a wooden saw and a dead hand are not flute and saw and hand because they do not function as flute and saw and hand; feathers and fur and scales are the same insofar as they have the same function. "Same" is different for the same beam, which is either a threshold or a lintel (1042b19–20, 26–27; 1043b9–10), and for the same brass, which is either a statue or a sphere, and for the same sight, which is either able to see or seeing. That entity is more primary which is more of an activity for its own sake and therefore not self-ceasing and which is not the actuality of . . . , not *ti kata tinos*, not *eidos to enon*, but form not of . . . and form not in . . . .

The most primary sense of being or entity is beyond the accesses to it both through the cyclic processes of the visible nonhuman order, especially the generation of animals and the locomotion of the heavens, and through the achievements of art and virtue, the excellences of production and action. Insofar as soul spans the difference between body (414a20–21) and the form of forms (432a2), it mediates between these accesses and quiescent mind. Minded soul contemplating form which is form of . . . and form in . . . frees that form toward the more primary way of being: being form only, being form alone. Separate entity in the most primary sense is the most primary sense of entity, the changeless which brings about change by being desired and imitated, unmoved mover beyond the otherness of a completeness anticipated or lost, and contemplation of what is most excellent, contemplation itself, beyond the otherness of scene, use, passion, friends, and deliberation about what will either come to be or not come to be, depending upon choice. Cosmic process and human production and action are underived from and irreducible to, yet overarched by the necessary and eternal actuality which they imitate in their difference from it, an actuality beyond instrumentality and futurity: separate and quiescent mind (*nous*) unmindful of human affairs. The divinely self-sufficient life of contemplation is better than life with others in action and passion (403a25). The anachoretic life *par excellence* is God, beyond courage and moderation, justice and generosity. No one would seem to wish for his friend the good of being God, for then friendship would cease. God does not order by commanding; the well-being of the best is without action. God and the cosmos have no foreign affairs. Take away from the living not only production but action as well; what is left but contemplation? Such is the joyful actuality of the divine (1154b26–28, cf. 431a6–7): excellent without respect-in-which (not excellent as horse or as carpenter, but simply excellent), knowing neither laborious nor interrupted and without teaching either received or given, ignorance without need to learn, quiescence without hebetude, solitude without loneliness: the most privileged sense of being or entity.

The doer and the doing of the deed are more one with the deed done than the producer and the producing of the work are one with the work produced, but the contemplator and the contemplated coalesce completely in that contemplating which is separate entity, form not said of anything and not in anything, achieving without background or result.

The popular opposition between Plato and Aristotle in terms of transcendence and immanence must be reformulated in the light of *Metaphysics* 997a34ff., 1040b27ff., and 1086b7ff., from which it is clear that Aristotle is concerned to work out a sense of separate entity, being neither cosmological nor anthropological, rejecting any sense that impugns separateness by doubling the beings with which we are familiar (Plato, *Parmenides* 130–35; Aquinas, *De substantiis separatis* no. 61).

Aristotelian cosmos has as its principle neither artificer nor soul, yet nature orders means as if it foreknew ends. The form of what comes to be by art is in the soul, but the forms of the cosmos are not in a factive soul. Natural forms are unmoved movers, neither coming to be nor ceasing to be, and natural motion (*entelecheia atelēs*) is the recapitulation of indwelling form. The fully developed offspring is prior to the seed from which it develops and prior to both is the generator whose form is the end of the generated. The making of nature is the cycle: reconciliation in eidetic identity of the priority of eternally anterior actuality with the priority of the eternally to be actual end; that which is to be or anticipated completeness is the anterior activity of the complete from which the seed proceeds (Siger of Brabant, *De aeternitate mundi* III, 42 Dwyer; Pomponazzi, *De naturalium effectuum causis seu de incantationibus* XII ad 8, Basel 1556, 298–317).

What is the relation between separate contemplation of contemplation and quiescent cosmic forms? How are the several senses of mind-which-makes related to perfective and unplurified mind without exemplary *logoi* (Proclus, *In Timaeum*, I 266.28–267.1 Diehl)? Pletho's polemic (*De platonica et aristotelica philosophia* XVII, PG 160, 909ff.) accuses Aristotle of falling into the impiety of Anaxagoras by denying nonhuman providential mind, and Aquinas's repetition of *Nicomachean Ethics* 1179a24–25 (no. 2133) is a correction (*In libros Physicorum* no. 974; *In libros Metaphysicorum* no. 2535; cf. nos. 2614-16 with PL 122, 458B: *vile*, e.g., *vermis*; cf. *De veritate* VIII 7). Lack of nonhuman providential mind is supplemented by human art and virtue, yet this art and virtue imitate the teleology of nature. Nature does not imitate art, but art nature; art is for aiding nature and for completing what nature leaves undone. Insofar as nonhuman order is craftsmanlike, the naturalness of human activities which order present affairs to anticipated excellences is saved without impugning the priority of eternal and impassible mind.

Logos spans the cosmological and anthropological accesses to silent mind (*nous*) (252a11–14, 639b15–17, 1253a9–10, 1332a38ff., 1334b15). The irreducible actuality of speaking together is the context of the art of drawing out implications of opinions, the art of giving reasons for facts (for saying that . . .) (1041a11, 15, 23, 25–26), and the thematization and justification of the presuppositions at work in any speech, a thematization and justification mediated by the use of speech to destroy speech (1006a25–26, 1007a19–20, 1008a31, 1025b28–30, 1041a14–15, b2–4). Although there can be no veridical speech about future chance and choice, poetic speech imitating action fills this space by limiting the indefinite context of preceding and succeeding actions (beginning and end) and by tightening the episodic sequence of actions to a likeness of organic necessity. This limiting and tightening fit action for contemplation, but for the sake of delight in constructed form, not for the sake of verisimilitude (1454b6–7, 10–11; 1460b1–2, 23–24; 1461b13–14) or of exhortation (1460b13–14). The character of the speaker and the passion of the hearer are powerful vectors in speech that moves to decision. Contemplative friendship or the sharing of speech in the knowledge of what is primary (997a11–12, 1141a20–22, 1170b10–13) is the highest form of the specifically human imitation of separate entity: science is of the necessary and eternal; and because the friend is another self, contemplation of a friend's contemplation is self-contemplation (Michael of Ephesus, *Commentaria in Aristotelem graeca* XX, 518–19).

The question of the relation between mind and teleological nature lies behind the question of the relation between the contemplative life of science insofar as it is an imitation of the necessary and eternal, and the political life of action insofar as it has a foundation in nonhuman order. Behind the question of the relation between contemplation and the city is a cosmological question: are the circlings of the heavens willed by star-souls with a sense of the sublunar or are they the natural movements of first body (Alfarabi, *The Philosophy of Aristotle*, 59.5ff. Mahdi)?

Does first unmoved mover mean mover of the first sphere? Are the many unmoved movers considered one principle, separate entity? Can nonbodily movers be many, not many instances of one kind, but numbered by the priority and posteriority of moved spheres one to another? The relation of separate minds one to another is understood in a cosmological, not an emanationist context.

Cosmic *erōs* for the actuality of mind is a crux: "if moved by desire, then besouled" (Theophrastus, *Metaphysics* 5a28ff. Ross-Fobes) (cf. 255a5–7, 285a29–30, 292a20–21). Human excellence or the life of the city longs for godlike deathless act, not as first body, imitating in cyclic motion the rest and joy of self-contemplation, swings the constellations, nor as sublunar nature, which works like a workman, works without the mind of a workman, but as speech with others longs for the perfecting silence of solitary *nous*. Nature is suspended from mind, and human excellences of word and deed are lived between them: nature teleological without anticipatory mind, mind contemplative without argumentative speech.

Another crux is the sense in which there is one science of entity, a science of the beingness both of any being and of that being which *is* in the most primary sense. Either the science of being as being is simply the science of the most primary sense of being; or the unity of the science is the unity of many senses of being said with reference to the one most primary sense, which as loved and imitated is the principle of unity; or the failure to achieve a science of separate entity forces radical inquiry back toward cosmology and anthropology, which are nevertheless known not to be concerned with the only senses or with the most primary sense of being. Some have even said that creation *ex nihilo* is the *sensus plenior* of the crucial text: "universal because first" (1026a30–31).

To say that deathless mind is caused with the generation of each human body, although that generation is not its adequate cause, cuts across the Aristotelian distinction between that which cannot cease to be because, being always, it has not come to be, and that which must cease to be because it has come to be (Theophrastus apud Themistium, *Commentaria in Aristotelem graeca* V/3, 102.24–29, 108.22–28). Creation, undermining the position that the union of generated body and ungenerated mind is less than essential, blurs the clear line between eternal mind and the imitation of that eternity by eternal coming to be and ceasing to be.

The subordination of nature to will, of nature as created nature to will as creating will, a reversal of Aristotle's deepest presuppositions and conclusions, began with the theological exploitation of his analysis of choice (H. Langerbeck, *Aufsätze sur Gnosis* [1967] 161; Philoponus on natural place and on the eternity of the world, *Commentaria in Aristotelem graeca* XVII, 581.18–21; X, 1333.23–27) and continued in Aquinas's use of his analysis of friendship for a theology of charity (*Summa theologiae* I-II, 65, 5).

Philosophers and Jewish, Christian, and Muslim interpreters of Scripture struggled over the anthropology of *nous*, God's liberality, His knowledge of matter and possibility, and His providence of chance and choice. Aristotle supplied theology with instruments of exposition, analysis, and polemic, but to the degree that these instruments were used for new ends this new use changed the sense they had in the hands of their forger and called forth restorations whose theological sense is to be indices of the gratuity of grace (Scotus, Prologue to the *Ordinatio* no. 12).

3

Providence and Imitation: Sophocles' *Oedipus Rex* and Aristotle's *Poetics*

I

King Laius and Queen Jocasta of Thebes have a son, Oedipus. The oracle of Apollo foretells that the son will kill his father. In order to prevent the fulfillment of the oracle, the infant's two feet are pierced and bound together, and he is given to the shepherd to be left on Mount Cithaeron to die. Out of pity the shepherd does not leave the child to die but gives him to a fellow shepherd, who in turn gives him to childless King Polybus and Queen Merope of Corinth.

Years pass.

A man who had too much to drink tells Oedipus that he is not the son of Polybus and Merope. Oedipus asks the oracle of Apollo at Delphi whose son he is. The oracle does not answer his question but says that he will kill his father and marry his mother. Oedipus, in order to prevent the fulfillment of the oracle, does not return to Corinth. Measuring the way by the stars, he goes to Thebes, where he cleverly solves the riddle of the Sphinx, saving the city from the Strangler, the One Who Binds. (The answer to the riddle is "man.") Oedipus is made king of Thebes, in place of King Laius, who, on his way to the oracle of Apollo at Delphi, had been killed at a place where one road becomes two (or two roads become one), killed together with all those with him except one, a slave who escaped.

Oedipus marries Jocasta, Laius's widow and the queen of Thebes.

A plague is destroying Thebes. Oedipus sends Creon, Jocasta's brother, to the oracle of Apollo. The oracle says that in order to save the city the murderer of Laius must be discovered. Oedipus calls down a curse on the one who has stained the city. Tiresias, a blind seer of Apollo, discloses to Oedipus that Oedipus himself is the murderer of the king and the polluter of the city. Oedipus suspects Tiresias of being used by Creon in a plot to overthrow him. Oedipus and Tiresias taunt each other's blindness with angry words. Tiresias calls the origin of Oedipus into question. Oedipus angrily accuses Creon of undermining him by false oracles in order to gain the city.

In deprecation of all oracles, Jocasta tells Oedipus that the oracle foretelling the death of Laius was false because Laius was killed not by his own son but by foreign robbers at a place where two roads become one (or one road becomes two). Oedipus remembers that on his way from Delphi to Thebes he killed in anger with a staff at just such a place. The slave who escaped is sent for; he is to say whether many or only one killed.

A messenger comes from Corinth to tell Oedipus that King Polybus is dead (and so the oracle of parricide seems false) and that Oedipus will be king of Corinth. But Oedipus fears returning to Corinth because of the oracle of incest. In order to quiet this fear, the messenger tells Oedipus that he is not the son of Polybus and Merope: many years ago the messenger himself gave them the child Oedipus. While shepherding on Mount Cithaeron he in turn had been given the child by another shepherd. The Theban slave who escaped the killing is that very same shepherd. The slave says that he in turn had been given the child by Jocasta, who wished it killed in order to prevent the fulfillment of the oracle. The outsider become king is shown to be born to the throne and to be the source of the stain by uniting with his origin.

Jocasta hangs herself.

Oedipus blinds himself. He still wishes to be touched and to touch. He goes with a staff, leaning and probing.

Creon will ask the oracle of Apollo if Oedipus is to be banished from the city of Thebes.

Thebes is cleansed. Both oracles are shown to have been true. The prophet Tiresias and the ruler Creon are vindicated.

II

What is the difference between the story of Oedipus and the work *Oedipus*? In the tragedy the events are not narrated, they are presented; more exactly, they are represented; they are not spoken about, but displayed; more exactly, they are played. The players who display the action, the actors who act out the action, are transformed and embellished by mask and costume; their words and gestures are transformed and embellished by meter, music, and dance. But it is the plot which is the soul and perfection (*telos*)[1] of the work. The action displayed in and through the plot is embedded in a matrix of antecedent

---

1. 50a22–23, 38–39 = *Poetics* 1450 Kassel.

and concurrent and consequent events which are not displayed; these events are either narrated or simply left out. The plot has a beginning, a moment artificially without antecedents, and an end, a moment artificially without consequents. Not everything that happens to someone or during a time is displayed; and nothing is displayed that happens merely after something: in the display what happens happens because of what has happened before. In the work nothing is left to chance, although in the story, in the matter of the artifice by which the poet constructs the work, a great deal happens by chance.

The work is an imitation of action. As an imitation of action, it limits the indefinite context of antecedent and concurrent and consequent actions, and it tightens the episodic sequence of actions to a pattern, a "syntax" (*systasis, synthesis*), an orderedness. The result is a completeness to which nothing can be added and from which nothing can be taken away, an articulated whole, neither too large nor too small to be well taken in all together by a gaze or a look (*eusynopton*). This completeness is a likeness of organic wholeness and necessity, a likeness of the wholeness and necessity in the relations of the parts of animals to one another. The limiting and tightening by means of the imitating work fit the action imitated in and through the work for contemplation which delights. This contemplation is not reducible to constating the verisimilitude of the work; much less is it for the sake of exhortation to virtuous action.[2] In what then do we take delight when we contemplate this imitation of action, this display of events in and through a work constructed by the artifice of the poet?

"Why should we honor the gods in song and dance (*choreuein*)?
"Why should we go to Delphi, the center of the world, . . . if concord between oracle and event be not displayed for all to see?"[3]

"It is rightly (*orthōs*) done when the poet misrepresents the way things are by presenting the impossible—if this happens because of the purpose and perfection (*telos*) of the work. . . . But not rightly, if not. . . ."[4]

The first quotation is from Sophocles' *Oedipus*; the second quotation is from Aristotle's *Poetics*. In the first quotation the chorus breaks out of the role it plays as the Elders of Thebes and speaks as itself, the means for representing or imitating the Elders of Thebes. (There is a moment in Aristophanes' *Clouds* that startles in a comparable way: the leader of the chorus steps out of the role he plays as Cloud and speaks as Aristophanes, the author—or as a facsimile of the author.)

---

2. 60b13–15.
3. *OT* 896, 901–2 = *Oedipus Tyrannus*; cf. *OT* 1086, 1094.
4. 60b23–28; cf. 33.

In the second quotation Aristotle is concerned with the casuistry of verisimilitude, with how we are to judge cases in which the imitation misrepresents the way things are. Comparing tragedy and painting, he gives two examples: a painter paints a horse with both right legs lifted up and put forward;[5] a painter paints a doe or hind with horns.[6] (Both examples are examples of misrepresentation of the animal world.)

What is the relation between these two quotations, the one from *Oedipus* and the other from *Poetics*? In order to understand the relation between the two quotations, consider the first quotation in the light of another quotation from *Oedipus* and consider the second quotation in the light of another quotation from *Poetics*:

"Zeus and Apollo, minding (*xunetoi*)[7] and knowing (*eidotes*) human affairs...."[8]

"Sweetening the work with other good things, the poet thereby covers over and keeps out of sight (*aphanizei*) the out-of-place (*atopon*) [whatever lacks *logos* (*alogon*)]."[9]

The themes of these two quotations are brought together by Aristotle in a single passage.[10] In discussing the use of "the machine," he speaks of events "outside the representation (*drama*), either having happened before, but being such that they could not be humanly known, or having not yet happened and being knowable only by prophecy. (For we hold that all things are seen by the gods.) There should be nothing *alogon* in the events, or if there be, let it be outside the representation (*tragōidia*), as in *Oedipus* of Sophocles.... It is necessary to imitate the skilled makers of likenesses: they reproduce the proper features or the look of the originals, at the same time making them look more beautiful."

To speak bluntly, there is no place in Aristotle's philosophy for the gods, although he recognizes and gives importance to the longstanding and widespread belief in the gods, and he calls excellent being and most excellent being "divine"; indeed, the most privileged sense of being he calls in an honorific way "god." But that most privileged sense of being has no knowledge of and no concern for anything lesser or lower than its own excellence; and a fortiori it has no knowledge of and no concern for the indeterminacy of choice and chance, the choice and chance which are so much a part of human affairs.

5. 60b18–19.
6. 60b31–32.
7. Cf. Heraclitus, fr. 114 Diels-Kranz.
8. *OT* 499–500; cf. 904: *mē lathoi*; 1191–92.
9. 60b1–2.
10. 54b2–11.

For Aristotle there is no truth about the future insofar as the future depends on choice and chance.[11] (It is not that the truth about the future is not known; there simply is no truth about the future to know.) The future is indeterminate and therefore unpredictable insofar as what will be depends on which of two alternatives, neither of which has yet been chosen, will indeed be chosen. And a chance event has no intelligibility of its own, but rather a borrowed intelligibility, an intelligibility borrowed from the intelligibility of the two teleological lines whose intersection results in the chance event. Virtue gives a kind of intelligibility to choice, and luck gives a kind of intelligibility to chance. We rightly expect the virtuous agent to choose in the future to do the virtuous deed, as he has done virtuous deeds in the past. This reliability of virtue lends intelligibility to the indeterminacy of choice, just as luck lends intelligibility to some chance events, insofar as a chance event is such that it could have been purposed, although it comes about by chance and not on purpose. Nevertheless, for Aristotle both choice and chance, and therefore the course of human affairs, lack intrinsic intelligibility.[12]

In *Oedipus*, on the other hand, an oracle has been spoken over future choice and chance; a word has been spoken, a *fatum*, a word that tells what the future will be. The action represented in *Oedipus* is the discovery that the oracle has indeed been fulfilled, that the word has been truly spoken. The discovery of the truth of the oracle vindicates the gods and cleanses the city. This prophetic word, which manifests the bond or nexus between past and future, comes from the gaze of the gods. There is a collecting look turned toward human affairs: there is a *xunon* and an *eidos* of human affairs. Providence,[13] foreseeing by a gaze or a look, makes possible prophecy or prediction, foretelling by a word. The gods "mind" human affairs: human affairs have the look of being looked at by the look of the gods.

In *Oedipus*[14] just before the reversal that comes about in the course of the announcement by the Corinthian messenger that the king of Corinth, thought to be the father of Oedipus, is dead, just before the

---

11. *On Interpretation* IX.
12. The intelligibility appropriate to (a) the artifact tragedy differs from the intelligibility exercised by (b) the virtuous agent (*phronimos, spoudaios*) and from the intelligibility thematized by Aristotle in (c) the book *Nichomachean Ethics* (1103b27–29). Each of these three intelligibilities is contrasted with its correlative lack of intelligibility: (a') the indefinite and episodic sequence of actions, (b') incontinent and vicious actions, (c') false "theories" about actions; cf. Kant, *Foundation of the Metaphysics of Morals* 404ff. and *Nicomachean Ethics* 1105b12–14.
13. *OT* 978.
14. *OT* 977–78; cf. 709, 723–24, 857–58, 946–47, 953, 971–72.

discovery that what seemed to show the falsity of the oracle has led to the discovery of the opposite, the truth of the oracle, just before Jocasta's recognition of the truth of the oracle, Jocasta, in order to quiet Oedipus's fear that the oracle could be true, calls on the rule of chance[15] and rejects providence (*pronoia*) together with the prophecy it makes possible.

In *Poetics* Aristotle, after recalling the opinion that the gods see all things, rejects the *alogon* in events insofar as they are represented in the well-made tragedy,[16] just as he bans from representation in the plot events related to one another by chance.[17]

It is wondrous, most wondrous, says Aristotle—and we delight in the wondrous[18]—when what is at first displayed and shown as being without *logos*, as happening merely by chance, turns out, against the first display and show (*doxa*), to have come about because of something else that happened before.

For Aristotle being is not episodic, like a poorly constructed tragedy;[19] being is not helter-skelter, not one thing after another without being because of another; being is not a mere heap (*sōros*).[20] The unifying plot of being, so to speak, is the eros[21] by which that which is less than excellent or not most excellent is drawn toward the most excellent. But the most excellent, because it is most excellent and therefore ignorant of the lesser and the lower, is without knowledge of human affairs in their indeterminacy. For Aristotle there is no nonhuman gaze, no divine gaze, no gaze of the gods in and for and through which the scatteredness and the indefiniteness and the fortuitousness, that is, the unintelligibility of human affairs, are drawn into intelligibility, that display of unity and definition and necessity for which there is no better word than *eidos*. For Aristotle the *eidos* of human affairs is an artificial *eidos*, the artifact tragedy, the plot constructed by the artifice of the poet. The gaze of the gods, the collecting gaze which binds together, the gaze which takes in what is past and passing and to come,[22] has for Aristotle no philosophical equivalent. But it is the unity of this gaze which the tragedy *Oedipus* celebrates ("Why should we sing and dance if there is no providence of human

---

15. Cf. the view rejected in *Physics* II, 8 & 9.
16. 54b5–7.
17. 59a24; 51b34–35; 50b32–33, 36.
18. 60a11–14, 17, 27–29; 52a4–7; 55a16–18.
19. *Metaphysics* 1076a1; 1090b19–20.
20. *Metaphysics* 1040b8–9; 1041b11–12; 1044a4–5; 1045a8–14.
21. *Metaphysics* 1072b3; 1075a18–19.
22. 59b19–20; cf. 59a32–33; 50b38–51a2, 4, 10–11; cf. *Politics* 1326b24; *Rhetoric* 1409a35–b4.

affairs?'"). For Aristotle the *eidos* of artifacts is in the soul of the artificer;[23] there is an *eidos* of human affairs, but it is not in the gaze of the gods; rather it is in the soul of the poet, the artificer of tragedy, tragedy whose plot adds necessities and sets boundaries and thereby excludes the too much and the too little, the indefinite. Aristotle says in speaking of "god," the most excellent and most privileged sense of being, that "there are some things it is better not to see;"[24] but tragedy displays for our eyes the obscene and speaks for our ears the nefarious.[25] Just as the indefinite is transformed by the limiting *eidos* of the constructed plot, and the fortuitous is transformed by the artificial "syntax" or orderedness according to which one represented event follows with necessity (or probability) what precedes it, so the obscene and the nefarious are transformed by the beauty[26] of the imitating medium. This transformation of the indefinite and the fortuitous and of the obscene and the nefarious is the Aristotelian equivalent of the "theodicies" of modern "philosophies of history." Plot is the artificial form of action: *mythos* is the artificial *eidos* of *praxis*. This is the Aristotelian equivalent of "philosophies of history," but it differs crucially from "philosophies of history" because this *eidos* of human affairs is artificial—and known to be artificial.

The plot constructed by the poet is neither a slavish copy of the action it imitates, nor an autonomous structure, a structure set up on its own as a law unto itself, a structure in its own right, freed from its model: plot is not "abstract" art. Aristotle understands imitation as something between these two extremes, copy or reproduction, on the one hand, and structure in its own right, on the other hand. Let us call that something between the extremes, for want of a better word, reflux.

The poet selects and organizes. The artifact he thus constructs gives unity and completeness, definition (*horos*)[27] and limitation (*peras*), necessity and orderedness to a scattered, indefinite, and loose "subject" matter. This selecting and organizing is the relation between the art of the poet and its matter, action. But because the constructed plot remains an imitation, an imitation of action, the artificial unity, definiteness, and necessity of the imitation reflux back on the imitated

---

23. *Metaphysics* 1032b1, 23; 1034a24.
24. *Metaphysics* 1074b32–33.
25. *OT* 1312; cf. 1224, 1334–39, 1430–31; cf. *Oedipus Coloneus* 1641–42.
26. 50b34ff. "The flute joins together the Gorgons (whose cries are imitated) and the Graces (from whose land come the reeds that make the flute); it is a blissful instrument for terrible cries." Kevin Crotty, *Song and Action: The Victory Odes of Pindar* (Baltimore and London: The Johns Hopkins University Press, 1982), p. 13.
27. 49b14; 51a6, 10, 15; 59b18.

action, thus unifying, defining, and ordering the action itself: the artificial imitation refluxes on the imitated action itself as imitated, as itself (re)presented in and through the unified, definite, and ordered imitation. The spectators gaze on action itself as (re)presented in and through the transforming and embellishing artifact constructed by the poet.

It is precisely because the discrimination of characteristics proper to the plot from the action imitated by and thus displayed in and through the plot is derivative and secondary that the artifice of the plot transforms the represented events themselves into an *eidos*. The action itself is displayed for us to see, but the action we see is heightened and sharpened by the means or medium in and through which it is there for us to see. The relation between the imitation and what it imitates is irreducible to verisimilitude, but this does not mean that the imitation is indifferent to the truth of what it imitates. The original is enriched, not distorted, by its image.[28] The imitated action is heightened and sharpened by the imitation into being more truly itself than it would be if it were not imitated and thus made available for contemplation in and through the transforming imitation.

What is displayed and that in and through which it is displayed are not split off from each other. Such a splitting off or amputation results in *membra disjecta*: "the aesthetic," on the one hand, and "the historical" or "the moral," on the other hand; but this modern opposition is foreign to Aristotelian imitation, which lives in the integrity of display and being displayed, show and being shown.

Tragedy displays the terrible, and this display of the terrible gives

---

28. For Aristotle the primary sense of *ousia*, the sense of *ousia* toward which all other senses tend, is *eidos*. Book Zeta of *Metaphysics* is the key to understanding *Poetics*. See *Metaphysics* 1030a6–9, b7–11; 1032a1–4; *sōros* ("heap"): 1040b8–9; 1041b11–12; 1044a4–5; 1045a8–14. What comes to be called "history" is a *sōros*; tragedy is an *eidos*. "... (things) drawn by art differ from true (things) by gathering together into one the scattered (things) (which are) separately..." *Politics* 1281b12–13; cf. *Metaphysics* 1065a24–26: *atakta, apeira*.

The tension between the imitating plot and the actions that the plot imitates is like the tension in Book Zeta between (a) form as form itself and not *kat' allou* (1030a11), not *en allō* (1037b3–4), form as *tode ti* (form "in some important sense a this"—but not a particular), on the one hand, and (b) form as form in matter, form as form said of matter ("in some extended sense a predicate"—but not a predicate said of a particular), on the other hand. See John Driscoll, "EIΔH in Aristotle's Earlier and Later Theories of Substance," in *Studies in Aristotle*, ed. D. J. O'Meara, Studies in Philosophy and the History of Philosophy, vol. 9 (Washington, D.C.: The Catholic University of America Press, 1981), p. 156.

As the subject matter action (*praxis*) is to the artifice plot (*mythos*), so *hypokeimenon* is to *eidos*. Cf. Pindar, *Nemea* VII 20–22: "... through sweet-speaking Homer the *logos* of Odysseus became more than what happened."

delight, the delight proper[29] to tragedy. How is it possible to delight in the terrible? The imitated terrible is *aufgehoben*, retained and transformed in and through the beauty of the imitating artifact which contains it, offering it as thus formed and transformed to a contemplation which delights in what it sees.

The expression "what it sees" is irreducibly ambiguous. It means as a unity both the moving and once-and-for-all-and-never-again action, the terrible action imitated, and the unchanging and repeatable imitation, the beautiful imitation in and through which the terrible action is imitated. Thus the delight proper to the contemplation of tragedy is delight in the terrible as displayed in and through a beautiful imitation.[30]

And just as delight is a kind of accompaniment of achieving (*energeia*), but sharpens what it accompanies and depends on,[31] so the artifact tragedy, the imitation of action, depends on its paradigm, action as lived, but this imitation adds a sharpness, a "point," to the imitated original which it thereby exceeds.[32]

Aristotle tells us that, because of an indefiniteness (*aoristia*)[33] of matter, natural processes lack teleological precision and that art sharpens (*epitelei*)[34] nature and brings it to completeness when nature itself fails to work through to its appropriate completeness.[35] Action too as lived lacks definiteness; but the art of tragedy heightens and sharpens action for display to mind avid for intelligibility, mind avid for unity and limitedness and connectedness.

Gazing on the artificial *eidos* of human affairs displayed in tragedy, this mind remembers the gaze of the gods, a gaze which has become for Aristotle only a longstanding and widespread opinion, a mere opinion shown up as such in the light of the rare knowledge of the most excellent and most privileged sense of being, separate mind unmindful of human affairs, separate mind knowing and enjoying its own excellence, that highest sense of being toward which human mind, which is somehow all things and not only the highest things, is turned in eros. It is this same eros which takes delight in the contemplation of the terrible in human affairs transformed by the form of tragedy.

29. 52b32–33; 53a35–36, b10–14; 59a21.
30. 48b10–11; 53b12.
31. *Nicomachean Ethics* 1174b31–33; 1175b13–14.
32. 61b13–14.
33. *On the Generation of Animals* 778a5–9; cf. *Metaphysics* 1037a27; 1065a24–26; *Rhetoric* 1409b2; cf. 51a17.
34. *Physics* 199a15–16.
35. *Protreptic*, fr. 11 Ross.

III

"What is drawn on a panel or incised on a tablet is both living (thing) [what-is-portrayed] and likeness: same-and-one and both [the two]; nevertheless the to-be is not the same to both, and there is gazing (*theōrein*) on [it/them] both as living (thing) and as likeness. . . ."[36]

All signs are irreducibly ambivalent; one sign is two: both signifier and signified. The sign (re)presents the signified in and through the signifier. Both words and pictures are signs; tragedy as an imitation of action is a sign that signifies action in a way that has something in common with the way words and pictures signify. Every signifier has characteristics of its own, characteristics proper to it, which are nevertheless in the service of signifying the signified.

The irreducible ambivalence of the sign consists in the polarity between "proper to . . . ," on the one hand, and "in the service of . . . ," on the other hand. The signifier is transparent in relation to its signified, but reflection can bring to the fore and discriminate the proper characteristics of the signifier, the structure it has in its own right.

To say that tragedy is an imitation of action is to say that tragedy is a sign whose signifiers are in the service of signifying the signified of tragedy, action. The proper characteristics of the most important signifier of tragedy, plot, are selection and organization, limiting and tightening, definition and necessity. Although reflection can bring to the fore and discriminate these proper characteristics for themselves, nevertheless, because they are first and primarily transparent in the service of (re)presenting action, they transform action itself as (re)presented.

36. *On Memory and Recollection* 450b21–23.

4

Notes on Nature

The City and the Garden

In the tension between ephemerality or oblivion (*lēthē, adoxia*) and memorable praise of shining excellence (*aretē*) is raised the question: which way of life is best?

That activity (*energeia*) is best which is the blesséd life of the gods, the divine, or God; and the best human life is assimilation to this exemplary activity. If the divine has knowledge of and care for human affairs, if providence can be said of it, if it minds the whole, if it is artificer and governor of the world, giver of laws and judge, then the best life is not without action, which implies the presence of others and concern with their good. The double or mixed life is best, imitating both divine knowledge of the world and divine action (*praxis*) toward the world. If there is community of gods and men, then public speech (*eloquentia*) and defense of fatherland are better than thought alone (*cogitatio*).

If, on the other hand, the divine activity is contemplation, contemplation of the most excellent only, of contemplation only, contemplation without production and action, activity beyond passions and companions, turned from and indifferent to the world, not troubling itself with the affairs of others, neither generous and benevolent nor avenging, if divine self-sufficiency (*autarkeia*), because it needs nothing, implies solitude, then the acme of the human as imitation of the divine is unpolitical contemplation: *tranquillitas beatae solitudinis*.

Agriculture is a commonplace for the themes of providence and chance, art and nature, publicity and hiddenness. To say that the life of political action is not the best life and that the cosmos beyond human intervention is better than the city is a protreptic to contemplation. Praise of the peace of rural life and flight from the busyness of the city imply that the natural and private is better than the conventional and public. The art of political life is rhetoric (*cedant arma togae*), but rural life is a *vita familiaris* of gardening: gardening is artful caring for the natural, an art necessary because untended nature does not sufficiently tend toward human ends. If the life of wisdom is without companions and action, then the life closest to it which is not yet wise is the quiet and hidden life of intimate friendship and unpolitical art: *hortulus amicorum.*

If in the beginning nature is fecund and beneficent without human art, if the archetype is the artless garden of delights, then nature is in principle caring, and political art as an art of caring for others is natural. But for that very reason there would be no need for human art, political or unpolitical; the divine shepherd cares sufficiently. Scarcity seems a sign of failure in nonhuman providence and a condition for human care: the Age of Cronos and the Age of Zeus. But the provocation of human art and law by lack and fault in nature is ambiguous, a sign either of absence of divine rule or of divine care for the specifically human.

> nequaquam nobis divinitus esse paratam
> naturam rerum: tanta stat praedita culpa.[1]

> ... pater ipse colendi
> haud facilem esse viam voluit, primusque per artem
> movit agros, curis acuens mortalia corda,
> neque torpere gravi passus sua regna veterno.[2]

But is busyness more human than freedom from work and office, ease for contemplation? The felicity of knowing causes is not idleness. Is there providence of that good not lessened in sharing: *theōria*? If God is only contemplative, then man cannot imitate him without first caring for a world left uncared for by the best, which does him good by causing him care.

Contemplation of the visible nonhuman order and especially of the order of the heavenly bodies depreciates human affairs and fame, and there is flight from artifacts and passing empires to eternal nature. On the other hand, we seek friendship with our own kind because we are strangers in an unwalled city: the blind and unbefriending world.

Nature and Gods in Epicureanism

Mathematics and single explanations of the motions of the heavenly bodies are suspect. Were there only one reasonableness of the visible nonhuman above us, then the indwelling or factive mind (world-soul

---

1. Lucretius, *De rerum natura* V 198–99.
2. Virgil, *Georgica* I 121–24.

or world-artisan) implied by this reasonableness would order human affairs as well, but with a providence oppressive in its necessity. A provident knower behind natural order would know and punish human disorder, and fear of punishment as well as concern with public order destroys peace of mind. Without such a knower there is no nonhuman exemplar for governing, the providence of man for other men. The best life is withdrawal from public affairs to nature, at the beginning of *De rerum natura* abundant and benign: *alma Venus,* whose embrace gives peace. *De rerum natura* ends with the Athenian plague, the bitter carelessness of nature for human affairs. Without the arts of agriculture and medicine, nature not only does not care but destroys. The inhospitable earth becomes livable only through hard work; all slowly sickens and falls to the worse; in the end death is stronger than any art. Free flight of mind toward what lies beyond the sundered walls of the world and discovery of the indifference of nature and gods to man are the true piety: *pacata posse omnia mente tueri.*

The *vates* celebrates a rite calling the man of war and empire to an archetypal peace (*apatheia*): the eternal fall of the indivisible and indestructible through centerless void without end: *per inane quietum.* The poem unites the soul with blind beginnings beyond all passion and care, pain and death. Were art and justice found again in the *summa summarum,* were making and ruling met again in the nonhuman, then the ceremonial and therapeutic passage to quietude would fail.

Touch is more fundamental than ungenerous sight: *invida praeclusit speciem natura videndi. . . . neque in lucem exsistunt primordia rerum,* nor do they laugh and speak. The poem is by artifice out of meaningless letters: the visible nonhuman order (*machina mundi*) is by chance out of dark and colorless elements. Origins are paradoxic or hidden, but the point of departure toward them is manifest: *musaeum dulce mel* and *natura daedala rerum.* Beyond the ephemeral manifest and in the knowledge that there is no nonhuman art and justice, to flee the city and live hiddenly is wisdom, assimilation to the irrefragable: lest we make all weak, shattering what is into nonbeing.

Et in Arcadia ego (death): the paean "we have lived well" accompanies contempt of those who cling to life. Beyond pastoral ease (*otium*) and the shores of light are the falling walls of the world and the peace of unending night.

Just as nature is without *logos* and *technē,* not depending on *mens* or *consilium* (*quod natumst id procreat usum*), so the gods are without public office (*aleitourgētoi*). But nature assures the concretion of the gods (*aeiphyeis*). Festive ascent to their quiet and carefree joy is salutary assimilation to paradigmatic blessédness come about out of the motion of passionless bodies in endless emptiness and beyond the passion of fear. The beneficent influence of the indifference of the gods to human affairs is generous nature's care for man.

The smiling and pacific gods are human, not spherical, in form, but without craft or office, anger or favor. Cult and blessing are to admire their ever-replenished excellences and to receive, in recollection of the fullness of past pleasure, which cannot be taken away, in public and customary rites and festivals and in common feasting and speaking together, a likeness of their calm and secure intermundane joy.

The sage, rightly understanding the nature of the divine, basks in a luminous fountain of salubrious images flowing from the holy bodies and so is taken into the company of the gods. Not only is the quiet harbor of the soul an assimilation to their virtue of turning away the harmful, but the suavity and openheartedness of friendship flower in likeness to their shared speech and their generosity without need.

Hobbes's Sovereign Teaching[3]

What transforms an avaricious and vainglorious one among others in the state of nature, pursuing his own interest in the light of his own judgment of good and evil and against the interests of such others together with him in the state of nature, into sovereignty, passionless and disinterested in its exercise, for the sake of the safety of the people, of its right to all and especially of its right to recognition as superior? The artificiality of being left alone in the state of nature (the artificiality of the isolation of the natural by covenant) and Hobbes's teaching as the measure of the exercise of the right of sovereignty to all, and especially of the right to recognition as superior, the right of each in the state of nature and therefore still the right of the sovereign insofar as he remains in the state of nature.

Hobbes's teaching as the specification of sovereignty's exercise of its natural right is natural public reason. Conflicting interests in the state of nature (for Hobbes the state of nature is such that all cannot be enjoyed in common and that to honor excellence is dishonorable) become reconciled under one exercise of natural right for the sake of the safety of the people, an exercise specified by the law of nature as taught by Hobbes.

3. The point made in this note began to become clear to me through a remark of Francis Slade of St. Francis College, Brooklyn: "For Hobbes, friendship is terrible."

The right to all, and especially the right to recognition as superior, of that instance of the state of nature which has been transformed into the right of sovereignty by the covenant of all other instances with one another becomes publicity or the city itself when the right of all others is restrained by the measure of justice and the refutation of ambition and when the right of sovereignty is exercised according to reason, that is, when, as the only remaining natural right, single and isolated because of the artificial limitation of the natural right of all others, it is measured by that promulgation of natural reason regarding things public which is Hobbes's teaching, a teaching whose power is the clarity with which it demonstrates itself as the only way to separate the desire for preservation and expansion from the consequence of violent death. Power is power to punish, and the punishment for being blind to the clarity of Hobbes's teaching is violent death. *Regum arx, pax populi, si doceatur, erit.*

The sovereign's right to all is not restricted by covenant; therefore he has a right to the death of anyone he wills to die. On the other hand, "No man is obliged by any contracts whatsoever not to resist him who shall offer to kill, wound, or any other way hurt his body." Tyranny and tyrannicide are left facing each other unless both sovereign and subject are ruled by Hobbes's teaching. The book *Leviathan* is the mortal god, the knowledge of good and evil.[4]

SUMMARY

The issue between ancients and moderns concerning the meaning of "nature" is focused on a comparison and contrast between Epicurus and Hobbes.

For Epicurus "blesséd" and generous nature has brought about a coagulation of atoms into the joyous serenity and exemplary freedom-from-care of a mortal god, Epicurus himself.

For Hobbes the "curséd" and niggardly state of nature is transcended through fear and by artifice. But there is no peace between the sovereign, who remains in the restless state of nature, and the citizens, who have covenanted only with one another and not with the sovereign, unless both sovereign and citizen obey the teaching promulgated in the book *Leviathan*, a mortal god.

---

4. *Vita, carmine expressa, authore seipso*, lines 249–50 (*Opera latina*, ed. Molesworth, Vol. I, p. xciv); *De Cive* II, 18; cf. *De Cive* II, 4; V, 11; *De Corpore Politico* (ed. Molesworth) I, 2, 3; I, 6, 10 = *Elements of Law* (ed. Tönnies) I, 15, 3; I, 19, 10; *Leviathan* XXVIII beginning.

5
A Reading of Augustine's *Confessions*, Book X

omni secreto interior, omni honore sublimior[1]

Aristotle's exclusion of action from the most primary sense of being, which because of its excellence is called "god," leaves a space for unsupported action, the space of human possibility: being able to be one way or the other and being within the power of the agent to originate by determining to be one way and not the other. In this space for choice and novelty, what we have decided and begun can never be undone, remaining perpetually unalterable.

For Augustine this space is taken up into a new sense of the divine: God does the unexpected and the unrepeatable; He is artificer and governor, craftsman and shepherd, lawgiver and caretaker, king and judge; He is partner to agreements; He promises and forgives, praises and blames, rewards and punishes; He is generous and avenging, merciful and just; He speaks in terms of passion and choice, construction ("the work of His hands") and convention ("the covenant with His people").

How is it that this is not a return to a mythology (stories of arbitrary intervention of the divine in human affairs: "give what you command and command what you will")[2] and a politics ("be our glory")[3] of

---

1. *Confessions* IX.1.1. quod legis ecce loquor, vox tua nempe mea est. *Vita S. Augustini episcopi*, auctore Possidio, 31 (PL 32, 64), quotes *Anthologia latina*, ed. Riese, I no. 721. Joseph Ratzinger, "Originalität und Überlieferung in Augustins Begriff der *confessio*," *Revue des études augustiniennes* 3 (1957), 375–92. Georg Pfligersdorffer, "Augustins *Confessiones* und die drei Arten der *confessio*," *Salzburger Jahrbuch für Philosophie* 14 (1970), 15–27. See *homologeō* in Kittel. Frederick J. Crosson, "Structure and Meaning in St. Augustine's *Confessions*," *Proceedings of the American Catholic Philosophical Association* 63 (1990), 84–97.
2. *Confessions* X.29.40 (twice); 31.45; 35.56; 37.60.
3. *Confessions* X.36.59.

wisdom? The Socratic accommodation to piety and law is repeated with a difference.

Does divine self-sufficiency exclude making and ruling? Is God either niggardly and a recluse or diffusive and a busybody? Can He create, command, and provide for others—for the lesser and even for the lowly—without suffering from the neediness of what He benefits and without Himself needing beneficiaries? Can there be freedom to choose without indeterminacy overcome and power to make without subordination to what is made, both freedom and power being one with eternal and necessary self-sufficiency?

Augustine is paradigmatic for the theological form of mind in contrast to the Greek philosophical form. Here is a hiding and a revealing of human mind in the creator God, who is free of all creatures and who lets creatures be because He freely wills them to be. The being of creatures is given in noncreaturely freedom and knowledge,[4] and human freedom and knowledge are ordered toward this noncreaturely free letting be of creatures out of nothing.

"God is all there is," although false, is meaningful for a sense of the being of creatures within the context of creation, which is free and out of nothing, that is, creatures are chosen by God as the alternative to there being only God. The plenitude of goodness would not be diminished, and goodness would not be impugned for lack of generosity, if creatures were not. Thus the goodness of creatures has a presupposition in relation to which it is questionable, although not denied. Questioning comes to rest in a freedom which could choose other than it does choose.[5] If God were to choose that creatures not be (because that creatures are is freely chosen, that is, chosen in fact although the alternative could be chosen, that creatures not be is possible, although contrary-to-fact), then all that "being" would mean would be God alone. On the other hand, for creatures to be is for them to be, without remainder or reserve, chosen by and manifest to another.

There is no longer any privacy: man is because he is manifest to another. But this publicity to God is as hidden as God Himself, unless

---

4. *Confessions* XIII.38.53; *De Trinitate* XV.13.22; *De civitate Dei* XI.10, XXI.8; *De Genesi ad litteram* VI 15.26–16.27, PL 34.350.

5. Scotus, *Ordinatio* 1.8.2.1. (Vatican ed. IV.324–26). Cajetan, *In quaestionem* XIX primae partis, in responsione ad quintum et quartum art. tertii (Leonine ed. IV.236; see Vatican ed. Scotus, VI.26*–30*). Bañez, *In quaestionem* XIX primae partis, art. 3, Tertio, Quarto; Ad tertium, Ad quartum; art. 10, Secundo, Tertio; Ad secundum, Ad tertium (Madrid–Valencia 1934) 414, 438, 441–42. John of St. Thomas, *In quaestionem* XIX primae partis, 24.2.35, 24.4.11*ter*, and 24.7.16 (Solesmes ed. III 76, 92–93, 132–33).

God's eloquence manifests Him as our public and as the friend who confirms us in our knowledge of ourselves and of one another. Outside this context public virtue or excelling in the eyes of others tends toward vainglory or pride of life, and private science or knowing for its own sake tends toward empty curiosity or lust of the eyes.

The *Confessions* are a dialogue between one man and God; they have the form of solitary prayer overheard, not of speech with others about being as it shows itself through city and cosmos. The Psalms are the origin of the rhetoric of the *Confessions*, a rhetoric whose form is *caritas*: *mutua redamatio cum quadam mutua communicatione et familiari conversatione*.[6] "Thus the Lord spoke with Moses face to face, as a man speaks to his friend,"[7] *garriebam tibi*.[8] Mind is achieved through first listening (*lectio*) and then speaking (*oratio*) to God, not through speech in the world with others. God is spoken to with words first spoken by God to us (prayer as quotation and appropriation of Scripture) and in the Word spoken in common with us (Christ, human and divine, Mediator).

What is best in the world is mind as abyss,[9] first hidden to itself and to others and then given to itself and to others through a manifestation of its manifestness to God. Man is freely confessing abyss in the image and likeness of the freely revealing hidden God. The Greek shining forth and manifestness to others has become hidden in manifestness to the hidden God, who through free revelation of His free creative knowledge reveals us to ourselves and to one another; *Deus conscientiae testis maxima est gloria*.[10] No longer Aristotle's "that which appears to all, that we call being,"[11] but rather "the hermitage of the hidden heart."[12]

We turn away from the speaking and the listening, the seeing and the being seen of citizenship and become strangers to one another in the hidden thoughts of the heart, being witnessed by the eyes of the Lord and moved in imitation of the Word to a new rhetoric: public witness or *confessio* before others.[13]

---

6. Aquinas, *Summa theologiae* I–II.65.5.
7. Exodus 33.
8. *Confessions* IX.1.1.
9. Aristotle, *Nicomachean Ethics* VI.7, 1141a34–1141b2; Psalm 41.8 Vulgate.
10. *De civitate Dei* XIV.28.
11. Aristotle, *Nicomachean Ethics* X.2, 1172b36–1173a1.
12. *Enarrationes in psalmos* 41.13, 55.9, 100.12, 134.16. *Sermo* 47.14.23, PL 38.311–12.
13. *Confessions* IX.4.8, X.2.2, XI.2.3, XIII.36.51 (*vox libri tui*). Cum oras . . . , os tuum in aure Dei est. . . . Cum vero legis, et os Dei in aure tua est. . . . Sive ergo tu loquaris Deo (quod utique facis cum oras), sive loquatur tibi Deus (quod tunc nimirum fit cum

The rhetorician Augustine goes to Milan and sees the preacher Ambrose: "when he read, he drew his eyes along over the pages, and his heart searched the sense (*cor intellectum rimabatur*), but his voice and tongue were silent."[14]

For Aristotle, mind finds itself in speaking with others about city and cosmos, although this speaking is implicated in a silence beyond public virtue and circular motion. But in the theological form of mind,[15] the heart can search the sense while the voice is silent because it is God speaking who manifests the sense of things. *Confessio*, speaking out from silence and manifesting forth from hiddenness in imitation of the freely revealing Word, overrides the Greek philosophical sense of the silence and hiddenness of the eternal and necessary by showing as paradigmatic, indeed divine, the free action of speaking for the ears of others and manifesting for the eyes of others. God is addressed with "give what you command and command what you will" and as the Other who, more intimate to us than we are to ourselves, confirms the availability of mind to itself and to others.

The impotence of mind to bring itself exhaustively from latency to patency and from dissipation to recollection opens it, seeking itself as manifest unity, to the one clarity of its creative exemplar. Solitary mind seeks to manifest itself to itself by itself.[16] But what mind is, is hidden in the hidden God. There is a cleavage between phenomenal and noumenal, between man insofar as he can show himself and be seen in the world by others and by himself and man as abyss, who is as being known by God, man who is whatever God knows him to be.[17]

Solitary mind, manifested to itself and to others as freely willed and willing in the sight of another, remains as a residue after the truncation and destruction of the theology which was the condition of the genesis of this form of mind. Mind, still remembering gratuitous participation in gratuitous creating and manifesting, tries to possess itself as enjoying the privilege of an Archimedean point exploited for mastery (the image is in Descartes's *Second Meditation*): mind offers itself the possibility of making itself in the world with others out of the

---

legis), . . . Guigo II, *De quadripertito exercitio cellae* 15 (PL 153, 827). "The *logos* goes forth from silence." Ignatius of Antioch, *Ep. ad Magnesios* 8.2.

14. *Confessions* VI.3.3, VIII.12.29 (*legi in silentio*), IX.4.8, X.6.9. Cf. Regula S. Benedicti 48.5. Jean Leclercq, "Lectio and Meditatio," in *The Love of Learning and the Desire for God* (New York, 1977), pp. 18–22. Bernard M. W. Knox, "Silent Reading in Antiquity," *Greek, Roman and Byzantine Studies* 9 (1968), 421–35. See no. 124, Bulletin augustinien pour 1969, *Revue des études augustiniennes* 16 (1970), 318–19.

15. Aquinas, *De potentia Dei* V.3, *In librum sententiarum* 1.38.1.5.

16. *De Trinitate* X.8.11.

17. Robert Grosseteste, *De veritate*, ed. Ludwig Maur, Beiträge zur Geschichte der Philosophie des Mittelalters, IX 1912.142.

solitude of its worldless freedom. Just as recollection of divine gratuity (the freedom to bring to be what would otherwise not be and what could be otherwise) is exploited in order to free freedom from the necessary, so recollection of divine exemplarity (the inexhaustible excess of unimitated imitability) is exploited in order to look down on being in the world with others as malleable.[18] The world we did not make becomes nothing but material for work; we return from solitude to being in the world with others to make a public to whom we display the solitude we left behind.

Deo uti: Descartes hints that the model no longer has primacy. Once imitators of the model, we now arrogate to ourselves the primacy of the model. The presuppositions of providence (being cared for by God) and miracle (being malleable in God's hands) are transformed into the presuppositions of technology. Pride in mastery replaces both admiration of excellence and gratitude toward generosity.

But God neither creates Himself nor needs creatures. Uprooted from eternal and necessary self-sufficient mind enjoying goodness, both freedom from natures and power over natures, which could be otherwise, and the glory befitting generosity and benevolence toward those who would be nothing without them, are monstrous fictions.[19]

SUMMARY

Book X is situated between the "autobiographical" Books I–IX and the "exegetical" Books XI–XIII, between Augustine's free recollection of himself out of forgottenness, out of hiddenness of himself to himself, free recollection for the sake of free self-revelation, and Augustine's interpretation of Scripture (the first chapter of the first book of the Bible), God's Word, God's free revelation of Himself as free creator, creator to whom He Himself and His creatures are exhaustively manifest, revelation of Himself and of creatures to creatures, creatures to whom God Himself and they themselves would, without that revelation, remain hidden. God's revelation of Himself and of His creature Augustine to Augustine is the Word in which Augustine is enabled to speak his revelation, his words freely revealing to other creatures what has been freely revealed in Scripture, in God's Word, to him about God and about himself: his *Confessions*.

18. Jeremiah 18.1–17.
19. Allan B. Wolter, "Native Freedom of the Will as a Key to the Ethics of Scotus," *Studia Scholastico-Scotistica* 5 (Rome, 1972), 359–70.

6

Creation, Solitude and Publicity

> Naturam expelles furcā, tamen usque recurret,
> et mala perrumpet furtim fastidia victrix.[1]

God alone, not choosing the possible alternative, to be alone, without looking to any other as model, using no material, and not enriched either by achieving the result or by the result achieved, gives others to be.

The one who is best creates, but creating is not what is best—the one who creates would be just as good if He did not create. Creativity and generosity-toward-the-lesser are not necessarily, although they are in fact, one with the necessary and self-sufficient one who is best.[2]

Nature, in the secondary sense, is creatures created by God; but nature in the primary sense is God—whether He choose to create or not to create, and therefore whether or not there be creatures at all, whether or not there be nature in the secondary sense.

If God were to choose that-creatures-not-be (that-creatures-not-be is possible because that-creatures-are is chosen as an alternative and

---

1. Horace, *Ep.* I, x, 24–25. "You can throw nature out with a pitchfork, but it will come back, breaking in unexpectedly, victorious over your perverse contempt."
2. Can God be necessary and generous without being necessarily generous? John of St. Thomas, *Cursus theologicus* XXIV, 4, Commentary on Aquinas, *Summa theologiae* I, 19 (Solesmes edition, III, 92b). "... quamvis esse illius actus volitionis et nolitionis sit necessarium et in actu secundo, tamen potest sequi habitudo non-necessaria: non propter esse actus, sed propter limitationem objecti quod sibi non est adaequatum, non minus in actu immanenti voluntatis erga objectum, quam in actu immutativo ad extra in objecto mutato: quia etiam actus immanens constituit illud in ratione objecti, et in ratione objecti contingentis, quia limitati et inadaequati sibi: totum enim objectum participat a voluntate Dei, nihil voluntas ab objecto. Et licet ille actus de se sit indifferens ad volendum et nolendum, immo sit ipse actus volitionis et nolitionis, potest tamen fundare habitudinem volendi potius quam nolendi ex se ipso: quia non habet indifferentiam passivam, quae indigeat alio superaddito ut determinate illam fundet, sed [est indifferentia] pure activa, immo et purus actus. Et ita ex se potest fundare determinatam illam habitudinem; sed quia erga objectum contingens et limitatum se habet, illudque tale constituit, ideo non necessario fundat illam."

chosen for no other reason than the choosing itself: the plenitude of goodness would not be diminished, nor would goodness be impugned for lack of generosity, if creatures were not), *then* all that "being" would mean would be God alone: the extreme of solitude.

The fact (that-creatures-are) to which the conditional (*if . . . , then . . .*) is contrary is the extreme of publicity: for creatures to be is for them to be both chosen by and manifest to another, the creator. Thus everything creaturely *is* gratuitously (creaturely to be is to be possible not to be) and nothing creaturely *is* secretly (creaturely to be is to be displayed).

If the creator chooses to manifest Himself to creatures, especially if He chooses to manifest Himself both as the one by whom creatures are gratuitously chosen to be and as the one to whom they are exhaustively manifest in their being, then some creatures, called to imitate in their freedom the creator, answer by choosing to manifest themselves to the creator and to one another both as chosen and choosing and as manifest and manifesting.

Publicity, choosing to manifest to others and manifesting choices determining others, becomes in the extreme both the gratuitous establishment of the plurality of being (the choice that-others-be) and the gratuitous revelation of the gratuitousness of this establishment—a gratuitousness that could have remained secret, the revelation of it being gratuitous[3]—and, in turn, free creaturely imitation of both this establishment and this revelation.

Hiddenness is thus manifested as the unchosen alternative to that chosen manifestation which does away with hiddenness. In overcoming hiddenness, manifestation brings to light the hiddenness that would have prevailed had it not been overcome.

The created thinking of the possibility that-creatures-not-be must include itself in this possibility and thus think itself both as being gratuitously willed by another and as being exhaustively thought by another.

The extremes of solitude and publicity first become meaningful in a theological context. When this context is weakened or ignored or attacked, but the extremes it made meaningful by conjoining them in the teaching of creation are retained, then there is modernity.

The rejection, in turn, of modernity takes two forms: either the return of the extremes to their theological context or the recovery of senses of solitude and publicity that have not been pushed to the

---

3. Creation (*ex nihilo* and *ex liberalitate*) seems in fact to have become known only through *ratio naturalis gratiā sanata*.

extremes, extremes conjoined in the teaching that God alone, not choosing the alternative and using no material, gives others to be: God-is-all-that-"being"-means is meaningful—although false—and all being that is not God is only because it is both gratuitously chosen by and exhaustively manifest to God.

But can we use the words "chosen by God" and "manifest to God" while cancelling, for what "God" means, the connotations "alternative left out" and "hiddenness overcome"? Lack? Triumph? God poor and victorious *ex parte connotati*?[4]

The Trinity is giving and receiving of plenitude, plenitude to which no created being could be adequate, plenitude given and received "without connotation" of anything created, generosity and gratitude "without connotation" of a possible but unchosen alternative, the alternative of not giving and not receiving in the sense of not creating and not being created.

And so the contingency said of the created, human nature of Christ is not said of the uncreated divine nature, although that contingency is truly said of one who is one of the Trinity, one in undivided, necessary and self-sufficient uncreated divine nature.[5]

SUMMARY

The theme is the relation between nature in the privileged sense and gratuitousness or generosity, that is, between God's self-sufficiency and necessity and His freedom to choose between alternatives each of which is equally good: first, whether or not God choose to cause creatures to be, that is, whether God choose to cause many others to be rather than to remain one alone; second, whether or not God choose to manifest to creatures the freedom with which they are caused to be, that is, whether God choose to disclose to others what would otherwise remain hidden. Solitude and secrecy in contrast to community and publicity are contrary-to-fact but meaningful.

4. "Considering the created-as-chosen along with uncreated necessity and self-sufficiency." "... actus purus cum connotatione ad aliqua volita, aut sine illa; et ex parte hujus connotati recipit contingentiam, non ex parte intrinsicae entitatis et perfectionis...." John of St. Thomas, *Cursus theologicus* XXIV, 2, Commentary on Aquinas, *Summa theologiae* I, 19 (Solesmes edition, III, 76b).

5. See Hans Urs von Balthasar, *Christen sind einfältig* (Einsiedeln: Johannes Verlag, 1983), pp. 106–7: *processio* and *creatio*.

7

Juxtapositions: Aristotle, Aquinas, Strauss

PREFACE

Leo Strauss is justly famous for the range of texts he interpreted and for the care given to the detail of those texts in interpreting them. This range and this care led to stressing the importance of the difference between "the exoteric and the esoteric" meaning of many of the interpreted texts; he has become notorious for stressing this difference.

The difference between "exoteric and esoteric" depends on two senses of "political philosophy"; the phrase "political philosophy" can mean both philosophizing about the political and the "politic" self-presentation of philosophy to and in the nonphilosophical realm of the political. (In Plato's *Defense of Socrates,* Socrates defends himself before the Athenian jury against charges of impiety and subversion by presenting his way of life as god-given and law-abiding.)

Each of the two senses of "political philosophy" depends on the difference between philosophy and the political. This difference in turn depends on the difference between the highest or the most fundamental things and human affairs; and this difference depends on the difference between necessity and self-sufficiency, on the one hand, and chance-and-choice (contingency) and being-with-others (community), on the other hand, and on the superiority of the first, necessity and self-sufficiency, to the second, contingency and community.

Together with "exoteric and esoteric" and "political philosophy," a third theme concerns Strauss: "ancients and moderns": the return from derivative ways of raising questions to the origin(s) of those derivative ways. This return finally leads back to Socrates. Socrates "never ceased asking the question 'What is . . . ?' about all the beings" and Socrates "brought philosophy down from heaven." The Socratic juncture of these two, the stance and the move, articulates the whole in a way that begins political philosophy. (Socrates, who wrote nothing, is accessible to us through interpretation of Aristophanes, Plato, and

Xenophon. Strauss gave a great deal of care to interpreting the texts of these three authors.)

Consider some passages from Strauss about Socrates, the articulation of the whole, the heterogeneity of kinds, the elusiveness of the whole, and political philosophy: *The Rebirth of Classical Political Rationalism* (1989), pp. 101, 132, 142–43; *Natural Right and History* (1953), pp. 122–23.

A fourth theme, the theme of this essay, concerns Strauss: the incompatibility between philosophy and taking creation to be true. For Strauss this incompatibility is based on a rejection of raising contingency and community, understood in a certain way, to a level higher than necessity and self-sufficiency, understood in a certain way (or ways).

This essay is divided into two main parts; each of these parts consists of thirteen parts: the first main part consists of thirteen quotations, and the second main part consists of thirteen formulations of positions of Aristotle, Aquinas, and Strauss.

PART ONE

1. "*meleta to pan*: Look to the whole."[1]
2. ". . . they are lovers of the gods and look to the divine in a certain way, the gods and the divine in which they believe because good things happen to them through chance."[2]
3. . . . that the gods are an evil, if a necessary evil. This would reduce piety to 'bearing the divine things as a matter of necessity'; . . ."[3]
4. "We cannot exert our understanding without from time to time understanding something of importance; and this act of understanding may be accompanied by the awareness of our understanding, by the understanding of understanding, by *noesis noeseos*, and this is so high, so pure, so noble an experience that Aristotle could ascribe it to his God. This experience is entirely independent of whether what

---

1. Periander of Corinth, *Die Fragmente der Vorsokratiker*, Diels-Kranz, 6. Aufl. (1951), vol. 1, p. 65.

2. Aristotle, *Rhetoric* I 17, 6, 1391b2ff. Cf. Leo Strauss, "On the *Euthyphron*," in *The Rebirth of Classical Political Rationalism*, ed. Thomas L. Pangle (Chicago: University of Chicago Press, 1989), pp. 202–3.

3. Leo Strauss, "The Birds," in *Socrates and Aristophanes* (Chicago: University of Chicago Press, 1966), p. 192. Cf. Leo Strauss, "The Problem of Socrates," in *The Rebirth of Classical Political Rationalism*, pp. 132–33, 142–43; "Thucydides: The Meaning of Political History," ibid., p. 101; *Natural Right and History* (Chicago: University of Chicago Press, 1953), pp. 122–25.

we understand primarily is pleasing or displeasing, fair or ugly. It leads us to realize that all evils are in a sense necessary if there is to be understanding. It enables us to accept all evils which befall us and which may well break our hearts in the spirit of good citizens of the city of God."[4]

5. "The God Who created heaven and earth, Who is the only God, Whose only image is man, Who forbade man to eat of the tree of knowledge of good and evil, Who made a Covenant with mankind after the Flood and thereafter a Covenant with Abraham which became His Covenant with Abraham, Isaac and Jacob—what kind of God is He? Or, to speak more reverently and more adequately, what is His name? This question was addressed to God Himself by Moses when he was sent by Him to the sons of Israel. God replied: 'Ehyeh-Asher-Ehyeh.' This is mostly translated: 'I am That (Who) I am.' One has called that reply 'the metaphysics of Exodus' in order to indicate its fundamental character. It is indeed the fundamental biblical statement about the biblical God, but we hesitate to call it metaphysical, since the notion of *physis* is alien to the Bible. I believe that we ought to render this statement by 'I shall be What I shall be,' thus preserving the connection between God's name and the fact that He makes covenants with men, i.e., that He reveals himself to men above all by His commandments and by His promises and His fulfillment of the promises. 'I shall be What I shall be' is as it were explained in the verse (Exod. 33:19), 'I shall be gracious to whom I shall be gracious and I shall show mercy to whom I shall show mercy.' God's actions cannot be predicted, unless He Himself predicted them, i.e., promised them. But as is shown precisely by the account of Abraham's binding of Isaac, the way in which He fulfills His promises cannot be known in advance. The biblical God is a mysterious God: He comes in a thick cloud (Exod. 19:9); He cannot be seen; His presence can be sensed but not always and everywhere; what is known of Him is only what He chose to communicate by His word through His chosen servants."[5]

6. "*The Prince* consists of 26 chapters. Twenty-six is the numerical value of the letters of the sacred name of God in Hebrew, of the Tetragrammaton. But did Machiavelli know of this? I do not know. Twenty-six equals 2 times 13. Thirteen is now and for quite sometime has been considered an unlucky number, but in former times it was

---

4. Leo Strauss, "What Is Liberal Education?" in *Liberalism Ancient and Modern* (New York: Basic Books, 1968), p. 8.
5. Leo Strauss, "Jerusalem and Athens: Some Preliminary Reflections," in *Studies in Platonic Philosophy*, ed. Thomas L. Pangle (Chicago: University of Chicago Press, 1983), p. 162.

also and even primarily considered a lucky number. So 'twice 13' might mean both good luck and bad luck, and hence altogether: luck, *fortuna*. A case can be made for the view that Machiavelli's theology can be expressed by the formula *Deus sive fortuna* (as distinguished from Spinoza's *Deus sive natura*)—that is, that God is fortuna as supposed to be subject to human influence (imprecation)."[6]

7. "Created good added to uncreated good does not result in something greater."[7]

8. "The communication of goodness is not the last end, but the divine goodness itself, out of love of which God wills to communicate that goodness [to others by creating]; for God does not act for the sake of His goodness as desiring to gain what He does not have, but as willing to communicate what He has, because He acts not out of desire for the end [not possessed] but out of love of the end [enjoyed]."[8]

9. "God wills the ordered whole of creatures for its own sake, although He also wills it to be for His own sake. These two are not inconsistent: for God wills that creatures be for the sake of His goodness, that they imitate and represent that goodness, each in its own way. This indeed they do insofar as they have [their] to be (*esse*) from that goodness and subsist in their own natures. Thus it is the same to say that God made [created] all things for the sake of himself and that He made [created] creatures for the sake of their to be (*esse*)."[9]

10. "How uncultivated and upstart is Scotus's way of speaking when he calls the divine will 'the first contingent cause.' It is nefarious to speak of contingency in the divine will."[10]

11. "If we were to take it that God had not willed the to be (*esse*) of creatures, for this reason we would not hold that there would be any imperfection in God, any potentiality in His being, but we would say only that there is freedom in the divine will itself and the lack of a certain 'relation of reason' [a term of art contrasting with 'real relation']."[11]

12. "The divine will, if it had not willed to create the world, would

---

6. Leo Strauss, "Niccolo Machiavelli," in *Studies in Platonic Political Philosophy*, pp. 223–24. (In the original "sometime" is one word and the last "fortuna" is not italicized.)
7. Aquinas, *Quaestio disputata de malo* V 4, ad 1.
8. Aquinas, *Quaestio disputata de potentia Dei* III 15, ad 14.
9. Aquinas, *Quaestio disputata de potentia Dei* V 4. (The manuscripts confirm the reading *fecerit*.)
10. Cajetan, Commentary on Question XIX of the First Part of Aquinas's *Summa theologiae*, Leonine edition, vol. 4 (1888), p. 236; cf. Scotus, Vatican edition, vol. 6 (1963), pp. 26*–30*.
11. Sylvester of Ferrara, Commentary on Book One, Chapter LXXX, of Aquinas's *Summa contra Gentiles*, Leonine edition, vol. 13 (1918), p. 224.

not be otherwise in itself than it is, having willed to create. But with the world itself it is otherwise: it makes a difference for the world when it actually receives to be (*esse*) from God and in its being is related to Him."[12]

13. "... the glory which comes to God from a more perfect or from a less perfect creature, granted that between the creatures themselves there is a great difference and that one is much better than another, nevertheless in comparison with God, to whom is infinite glory of Himself, this difference in extrinsic glory given (or not given) by a more perfect creature adds nothing of moment. The whole of creatures all together, in comparison with God, is to be taken as empty, a nothing, as it were, a drop of dew before sunrise."[13]

PART TWO

1. For Aquinas although God knows and wills many and other beings and in that sense is not solitary, nevertheless it is meaningful although not true that God be the only sense of "being" and that "being" mean not God and many others as well but God alone.

2. For Aristotle separate being in its self-sufficiency does not contemplate lesser beings and does not choose lesser beings, but separate being could not be the only sense of "being." It is necessary that "being" mean being in common to many and being in common with others.

3. For Aquinas God can annihilate *ex simplici voluntate* creatures that are necessary insofar as they are beings of a nature in which there is no principle of the possibility of ceasing to be, and God knows the actuality of the contingent future in its presentness: *prout est in esse suo determinato*.[14]

4. For Aristotle necessary natures are eternally actual, and the contingent future is able not to be going to be.

5. Aquinas crisscrosses the Aristotelian positions, holding the annihilability (*possibilitas ad non esse*) by God of necessary natures and the actuality (*esse determinatum*) for God of the contingent future.

6. This crisscrossing is a miscegenation between necessity and con-

---

12. Bañez, Commentary on Question XIX of the First Part of Aquinas's *Summa theologiae* (Madrid–Valencia, 1934), p. 442.
13. John of St. Thomas, Commentary on Question XIX of the First Part of Aquinas's *Summa theologiae, Cursus theologicus*, Solesmes edition, vol. 3 (1937), p. 133a; see also pp. 76b, 92b; further, Wisdom 11:22; *Summa contra Gentiles*, Book Two, Chapter II, tertio.
14. See Aquinas, *Quaestio disputata de potentia Dei* V 3 and *Scripta super libros Sententiarum* I 38, 1, 5.

tingency, the parts into which the whole is articulated—if the last transcendence is the transcendence of the whole to its parts, and if the last immanence is the immanence of the whole to its parts. But if there are three transcendences? The transcendence of the better part of the whole to the less good or lesser or lower part of the whole; the transcendence of the whole itself to all its parts; and the third and last transcendence, which transcends the whole and is immanent to it without being together with it another and better and last whole.

7.

God

```
        ┌──────────────────────────────────┐
        │ necessity₁ and self-sufficiency₁ │
        └──────────────────────────────────┘
                    ╱  ↑  ╲
   freedom of indifference to create or not to create
                  ╱    ↓    ╲
        ┌──────────────────────────────────┐
        │ necessity₂ and self-sufficiency₂ │
        ├──────────────────────────────────┤
        │    contingency and community     │
        └──────────────────────────────────┘
```

the created whole

8. For Aquinas God and creatures together are not the last whole. As part of a whole, one part is complemented by another part, no matter how much more excellent the one is than the other. God is not complemented or completed by any other. This is the meaning of the freedom of indifference to create or not to create. God as necessity$_1$ and self-sufficiency$_1$ transcends or exceeds the whole whose parts are necessity$_2$ and self-sufficiency$_2$ and contingency and community. God is as immanent or intimate to the lower part of the whole (contingency and community) as to the higher part of the whole (necessity$_2$ and self-sufficiency$_2$). Necessity$_1$, not part of the whole, is freedom of indifference to necessity$_2$, the higher part of the whole, and necessity$_1$ establishes contingency, the lower part of the whole, in its very contingency.[15]

9. For Strauss the best is the whole within which necessity$_2$ and self-sufficiency$_2$ are the better part and contingency and community the less good or lesser or lower part. Thus for Strauss necessity$_1$ is assimilated to necessity$_2$, the better part of the whole, and freedom of indifference to create or not to create is assimilated to contingency, the less good or lesser or lower part of the whole.

---

15. See Aquinas, *In libros Peri hermeneias expositio* I 14, 22; *In Metaphysicam Aristotelis commentaria*, ed. Cathala, nos. 1220–22.

10. For Aquinas God Himself as necessity$_1$ and self-sufficiency$_1$ is freedom of indifference to whether or not (this looks like contingency as indeterminacy) there be many others (this looks like community as complement), to whether or not there be the created whole, whose parts are necessity$_2$ and self-sufficiency$_2$ and contingency and community. God's freedom to create or not to create is not indeterminacy or arbitrariness in Himself, but the necessity and self-sufficiency of His goodness, which cannot be complemented or completed by any other and which cannot be assimilated to either part of the created whole.[16]

11. For Strauss so-called divine chance-and-choice and so-called divine being-with-others are assimilated to contingency and community, the less good or lesser or lower part of the whole, the part which, although inferior, is, as a part of the good whole, as a part of the whole as good, nevertheless indispensable to the goodness of the whole. Contingency and community and necessity$_2$ and self-sufficiency$_2$ are the two parts of the whole. The whole is better than the better part, necessity$_2$ and self-sufficiency$_2$. Contingency and community, the less good part of the whole, make the whole better than it would be without that lesser or lower part. In that sense, contingency and community are "divine." They contribute to the goodness of the whole, which would be less good without them. The higher is better than the lower, but the best is the whole, both the higher and the lower together. The whole is divine in the proper sense. Contingency and community are called "divine" only because they contribute to the divine in the proper sense, the whole, the good whole, the whole as good, the goodness of the whole.

12. For Aquinas the superabundant and therefore necessary and self-sufficient goodness of God is His freedom, freedom without indeterminacy or arbitrariness, freedom that is free-of-and-for whether or not there be many others, freedom that is free to be generous because, being self-sufficient, it need not be generous.

13. For Strauss the Covenant and the Law and the Prophets are assimilated to chance-and-choice and being-with-others, which are the less good or lesser or lower part of the whole. Chance-and-choice and being-with-others are an indispensable and in that sense necessary part of the last and in that sense self-sufficient whole.[17]

---

16. Miracle is less proximately but more precisely (cf. Aristotle, *Metaphysics* 982a25–28) characterized as motivating the move from nature$_2$ to nature$_1$ than as motivating the move from nature$_2$ to choice, the choice that chooses the way creatures are, the choice whose principle is nature$_1$.

17. "This, then, will be a key permitting one to enter places the gates to which were locked. When those gates are opened and those places entered, the souls will find rest

SCHOLIUM

Taking creation to be true is for philosophy not a repudiation of the primacy of nature over convention; much less is it a fall back from the difference between nature and convention into "the ways" prior to the differentiation of nature and convention.

Philosophy, as eros for nature and for the whole, is not less itself (a) for moving from a less primary sense of nature, nature_2, to the most primary sense of nature, nature_1, most primary because of its eternity and necessity, self-sufficiency and intelligibility, and (b) for moving from the whole to the principle of the whole, the principle that is not itself a part of the whole.

---

therein, the bodies will be eased of their toil, and the eyes will be delighted." Maimonides, *The Guide of the Perplexed,* "Introduction," *in fine.*

8

A Reading of Hume's *A Treatise of Human Nature*

I

Hume's *A Treatise of Human Nature* is an experiment, the experiment of following an attraction to its end, the attraction of autonomy unmixed with heteronomy.[1] What would remain of human nature after the elimination of belief without evidence (freedom from the heteronomy of obscurity) and after the elimination of rule over desire (freedom from the heteronomy of restraint)? Is being human compatible with hyperbolic evidence, evidence not intertwined with obscurity? Is being human compatible with rampant desire, desire not put down by law? Is being human compatible with unspeaking mind and with unruled passion? Can human nature be freed from heteronomy: theoretical obscurity and practical restraint? Enlightenment is put to the test.

Hume gives a *modus tollens* argument for belief in the unity of things in the motion of their manifestations, for belief in the unity of selves in the motion of their experiences, and for rule over the passions of vanity and avarice (the desire to be more than others in the opinion of others and the desire to have more of what cannot be enjoyed by one if it is enjoyed by another). The argument shows that neither free-floating impressions (free-floating because underived, unappropriated, uncombined: neither presence of . . . nor presence to . . . nor

---

1. This is only a statement, not an argued statement, of a reading of Hume's *A Treatise*. Let the reader take it in hand as a template or a *vade mecum* when rereading what Hume himself has written. This interpretation of Hume continues and complements "Ancients and Moderns: Notes On Interpreting Hume," in Studies in Philosophy and the History of Philosophy, vol. 4, ed. John K. Ryan (Washington, D.C.: The Catholic University of America Press, 1969), pp. 67–74. (Familiarity with the interpretations of Hume by Thomas Hill Green and Norman Kemp Smith is presupposed.) See also Donald W. Livingston, *Hume's Philosophy of Common Life*, Chapter 1 (Chicago: The University of Chicago Press, 1984).

presence with . . .) nor community of scarce goods can be both lived and formulated. (Free-floating impressions might be lived without being formulated in being lived.[2] Community of scarce goods might be formulated without being lived in being formulated.[3]) The argument is reduction of pure theoretical autonomy to silence and reduction of pure practical autonomy to violence. Free-floating impressions are silent because speech corroborated by evidence is achieved in a unity uniting the difference between speech and what is spoken about, between speech and speaker, and between speech being spoken and speech already or not yet spoken. ("Free-floating" means freedom from union with any other.) Community of scarce goods is violent, each one desiring to make his own alone what is also another's but cannot be enjoyed by both together and so must be taken away from another in order to be enjoyed by one: war of each against all. The extreme of contemplation, the silence of free-floating impressions, cannot be brought into a unity of being both lived and formulated. Nor can the extreme of passion, the violence of vanity and avarice in the community of scarce goods, be brought into a unity of being both formulated and lived. There cannot be theoretical and practical speech, assertion or denial and praise or blame, if impressions have not faded into the obscurities and combined into the unities necessary to belief in things and in selves, and if passions have not been checked by the manners necessary to a peaceful community. Assertion or denial and praise or blame, and therefore Hume's *A Treatise* itself as an instance of theoretical and practical speech, would be self-destructive if there were freedom from the heteronomies of obscurity and restraint. *A Treatise*, insofar as it is a work of sustained argument and a work attributed to an author continent in character, shows as such a work so attributed that being human (in the sense of being both a consistent speaker anticipating and recapitulating speeches and a respectable agent praising and blaming actions) is impossible without obscurity and restraint.

But the line of argument is unclear and the author's character is questionable when Hume not only speaks about that-which-is-not, evoking the hypothesis of being human without obscurity and restraint, but also speaks in the role of an advocate of the hypothesis of theoretical and practical extremes, being human without obscurity and restraint, extremes which cannot be advocated without in that very advocacy performing as a speaker consistent with himself and

---

2. Aristotle, *Metaphysics* XII 7, 1072b26–28.
3. Aristotle, *Politics* II 5, 1263b16–18, 23–25.

respectable to others. And so *A Treatise* itself, insofar as it is authored and addressed by a speaker both consistent and respectable, is evidence for obscurity and an example of restraint.

In what role does Hume speak when he speaks of these as fictions: (a) the continuity and independence of the visible when vision is interrupted, and (b) justice and property? In a role determined by positions taken as somehow natural: (a) only seeing is believing, and (b) goods in common lead to war. But these positions explode if forced toward a unity of being lived and formulated or formulated and lived. The natural so understood is self-destructive in favor of fictions.

Can discourse be true if in the discourse its author dissolves himself into separate impressions? Can discourse be good if in the discourse its author represents himself as standing in vanity and avarice against others? Would human nature remain without true and good discourse? (Although the humanly true is inseparable from obscurity and the humanly good is inseparable from restraint, the humanly true is not arbitrary and the humanly good is not repressive.) Constancy and continuity, coherence of things and of selves, and peaceful community of owners with manners are reestablished beyond the bright and hot fires of hyperbolic evidence and rampant desire: separateness is corrected. But, after the vindication of obscurity and restraint, what distinguishes enlightened opinion from the arbitrariness of reverie, caprice, prejudice, credulity, superstition, enthusiasm, madness? What distinguishes enlightened convention from law masking repression?

II

Nature hides itself; nature, taken in one sense (nature$_2$), hides nature, taken in another sense (nature$_1$); nature is ambiguous. Nature$_2$, belief and sympathy (synthesis of many perceptions into perceptions of one thing, synthesis of many perceptions into perceptions to one self, synthesis of present perceptions with perceptions past and future, and synthesis of myself with other selves), corrects nature$_1$, perceptions without synthesis and private interest in common goods.

A Treatise, insofar as it is a consistent and respectable work, presupposes the correction of nature$_1$ by nature$_2$. *A Treatise* presupposes both a common world, beyond differing perspectives and irreducible to interrupted perceptions of nothing to nobody, and address to others by an author with a character not vain and avaricious.

A Treatise shows nature$_2$, the presupposition of the performances that achieve *A Treatise* as a consistent and respectable work, as the correction of nature$_1$, the presupposition of the separateness of perceptions (perceivings not only separate from a perceived and from a perceiver but also from one another) and of the privacy of interest in what is common (each making use of his right to all and over all). A *Treatise* shows the ambiguity of nature by showing nature$_2$ against the foil of what would be if nature$_2$ did not overcome nature$_1$ by belief and sympathy.[4]

Without the correction of nature$_1$ by nature$_2$ there would be only a monster, lonely and rapacious, come of the union of the actuality of perceiving without perceived and without perceiver, a solitary and quiet unity (*nous*), with the war of each against all in the desire for more (*pleonexia*).

Nature$_1$ is always already overcome, surpassed, covered over. Nevertheless, Hume uncovers this correction of separateness and speaks about what is under the overcoming, the surpassing, the covering over: he lets be seen what would be if not; he lets us see that-which-is-not. In doing this he leaves everything as it is, corrected, yet after the showing we are not the same as before. We have learned to recognize belief and sympathy (which have never been denied as presuppositions of the performances that achieve a consistent and respectable treatise) as corrections of what is not available to us except as that-which-is-not, because without the corrections we would have to live in silence and to speak in violence: we would not be of human nature.

III

A Treatise of Human Nature is ambiguous, as nature, its presupposition and theme, is ambiguous.[5] This ambiguity reminds us that for Aristotle argument is not without motion and opponents, as war is for the sake of peace, and also that for Aristotle there are knowing not derived from argument, virtue (*sōphrosynē*) beyond continence, and goods in common without contention.

For Aristotle neither nonhuman separate mind nor community of contemplative goods, goods which can be given without being lost to the giver, have within themselves springs of alienation: othering. Con-

---

4. Regular association of ideas, and self-interest tempered by calculation of effectual means are the first stage in liberation from silent and violent autonomy: liberation from theoretical and practical isolation (atomism of evidence and desire) toward coherence of things and toward community of speakers and agents. The second stage of this liberation is necessary connection ("causality") and disinterested approbation ("moral sense").

5. Propensity to fictions is more natural than the niggardly nature it supposes and covers over: Hume reverts to the benevolence of nature by first supposing and then covering over the malevolence of nature.

templation need not be transcended toward belief, and community of goods need not be transcended toward modesty and property—if the contemplation is nonhuman and if the shared goods are contemplative.

For Hume both mind as separate impressions (uncollected timeless flashes illuminating nothing for no one) and war over noncontemplative scarce goods in common (a savage and wretched state) are othered by belief and by modesty and property. Hume's weakening of contemplation as unmoved mover is mirrored in his weakening of the community of contemplative goods, which he replaces by conventional division and limitation and by artificial multiplication and expansion.

For Aristotle the best of the practical, friendship, leads beyond itself toward the nonhuman contemplative, contemplation without othering. For Hume the best of the human contemplative, impressions, leads beyond itself toward the practical, manners and industry.

9
Husserlian Distinctions and Strategies in *The Crisis*

> Moving forward and looking ahead,
> coming closer to what lay behind,
> I saw it grow larger and larger.

> ... Aufklärung der Geschichte in Rückfrage
> auf die Urstiftung der Ziele ...
> (VI 72, 31–32).*

Husserl uses the perception of bodies as a model to articulate and clarify confused and obscure senses of mind. His analysis of the perception of bodies is in terms of the difference between different acts of meaning which mean the same meañt, between the act of meaning and the meant, and between merely meaning-acts and the synthesis of meaning-act and manifesting-act (this synthesis itself can in turn be meant and manifested). He analyzes in terms of act and manifestation:

(1) I hold sway over my perceptual fields and over themes within fields: *Inszenierung*; *ins Spiel setzen*; *"Bilder" sich einstellen lassen*.

(2) One and the same manifested is manifested from many and different perspectives and in and through many and different aspects.

(3) Manifestation is a shift from meant'-and-not-yet-seen (and meant"-and-seen) to meant'-and-seen (and meant"-and-no-longer-seen). (Seeing is in terms of a usually unthematic but nevertheless operative and thematizable web of meaning.)

Husserl transposes (*mutatis mutandis*: 1/1', 2/2', 3/3') this analysis of the perception of bodies to nonperceptual themes and manifestings:

---

*References are to volume, page, and line of *Husserliana*.

(1') Belief is a nonperceptual theme. Holding sway over my interests and themes, I can shift from belief' in a believed-in' to belief" only in that belief', which becomes through this shift believed-in". Belief in a body is not that believed-in body, and I can shift my interest from the believed-in body to the belief in the body. And to state that someone believes that . . . is not to state that . . . , although it usually implies understanding what ". . ." means.

The act of quoting my' own speech about my' believed-in world establishes a new sense of *I* (I") distinct from the sense of *I* (I') implied in my' own. The bourdon of belief' in believed-in' continues after the shift that thematizes belief' as believed-in", believed-in" by me" and spoken of by me" (I 72–75; VIII 79, 15–16).

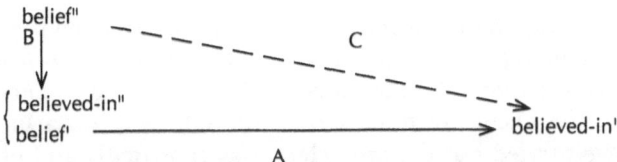

(To exclude C is not to interfere with A; within the psychological reduction both A and B are at work; within the transcendental reduction only B is at work.)

(3') There is a teleology toward synthesis with manifesting acts of acts which mean that which cannot be seen at all.

There are acts of meaning that mean without any apperception of anything to be manifested in and through many and different sides, some side always being not yet seen or no longer seen. ("Apperception of . . ." means here an unthematic but nevertheless operative and thematizable belief in . . .) (XI 336–45).

We can speak of a theorem itself because the one theorem cannot be reduced to the many thinkings of it, the many thinkings by which the same thinker and different thinkers return to the same theorem again and again.

What is at issue itself (*die Sache selbst*) as the term of a manifesting-act is also as the same (*die selbe Sache*) the term of merely meaning-acts preceding or succeeding that manifesting-act in the time-stream, and thus, through the unity of the time-stream, what is at issue as manifested has itself as unmanifested as context.

Manifestation cannot be reduced to expansion of context, thematizing the unthematic but nevertheless operative web of meaning within which the manifested is embedded—this expansion itself is a manifestation (*Abhebung*) which manifests the anticipation of a manifestation.

(2′) There is a synthesis of acts of meaning and manifesting which is different from the synthesis of many and different acts in one and the same meant and manifested. This synthesis is the intentional unity formed by the form of temporality: impression distended in retention and protention. This form forms itself (presencing itself is absenced and presenced out of absence), and the unity of the form as forming itself and the form as formed by itself is the unifying form of all that which is present as distended in the time-stream (the phasal structure of immanent unities: states of sensibility and interpretations of those states as manifestations of transcendences; acts of reflection).

Husserl works toward a sense of mind ("transcendental subjectivity") such that the science of mind is the science of *hen panta,* one theme which gathers all other themes. Mind is to be understood in this sense: if a science of mind were achieved, then this achievement would have carried out the task which was confusedly and obscurely anticipated in the originating sense of philosophy. Such an achievement ("a regulative idea") would fill the empty intention established in the origination (*Urstiftung*) of philosophy.

Here we ask two questions of Husserl:

(1) Why the prevenient alienation and obfuscation of transcendental subjectivity into anonymity and naïveté? Why the fall into a condition in which and out of which there must be an origination of the sense of the task of overcoming this anonymity and naïveté? Why do we begin from being taken up with the world and from being unmindful of the web of beliefs at work in meaning a world at all?[1]

"Phänomenologische Auslegung ... tut ... nichts anderes ... als den *Sinn auslegen, den diese Welt für uns alle vor jedem Philosophieren hat und offenbar nur aus unserer Erfahrung hat, ein Sinn, der philosophisch enthüllt, aber nie geändert werden kann* und der nur aus Wesensnotwendigkeit und nicht aus unserer Schwäche in jeder aktuellen Erfahrung Horizonte mit sich führt, die der prinzipiellen Klärung bedürfen" (I 177, 4–22; 192, 11–13).

Appearings themselves can appear (as that which appears and not as appearings of that which appears) only in contrast with a back-

---

1. Perhaps the question presupposes a misunderstanding of the transcendental as *hinterweltlich* and of constitution and reduction as *próodos* and *epistrophē.* "Non-worldly" (with hyphen) indicates transcendental but not *hinterweltlich.*

ground: themselves as the appearings of that which appears preveniently.

(2) Is it possible that the originating sense of philosophy as anticipation of the science of *hen panta* would explode into nonsense (*Widersinn*) were we to try to bring that sense from confusion and obscurity to articulation and clarity?

The achievement of that science would be inseparable from the achievement of a body of appropriable discourse, and any appropriator of that discourse would be formed by *die lebendige Gegenwart*; thus the anticipation of that achievement must be the anticipation of recapitulation and anticipation. Presencing distended is the form of any achievement of articulation and clarity.

Husserl exhibits the inadequacies of two claims to a science of mind:

(1) Psychology burdened with the transcendental task, a psychology that attempts to take the transcendental turn within belief in the world. Here "world" means either (a) the believed-in system of whatever is manifestable in and through sides (this system is compact but to be articulated endlessly) or (b) at least the apperception of something manifestable in and through sides.

(2) Psychology modelled on the mathematical science of nature.

Husserl attacks the claim that there can be no science of mind, but only collation of world-views. This claim has a weaker form: there can be no science of whatever sense of mind is left over (*"fortgeworfenes Abschnittsel"*) (IX 55, 1–7; 156, 17) from psychology modelled on the mathematical science of nature.

The mathematical science of nature takes over the claim to universality from the originating sense of philosophy ("the science of *hen panta*"), but in attempting to make good that claim it is limited by the apperception of natural ("worldly") cores. (This apperception is compatible with the algebraicization of cores.)

The crisis results from two confusions, both of which result from differentiating a new sense from a matrix but at the same time not setting the new sense free from the matrix from which it is differentiated:

(1) The confusion of non-worldly world-constituting subjectivity with subjectivity at work within the already constituted world.

(2) The confusion of mathematics which has bracketed all natural cores with mathematics which still apperceives natural cores.

The crisis has a Cartesian root because Descartes anticipated the nonnatural sense of both subjectivity and mathematics, but he did not sufficiently purify the nonnatural sense from contamination by the implicit exercise of belief in bodies.

World, in the loose sense, implies apperception of the transcendent, that is, of one and the same meant as standing over against and not being part of the stream of many and different acts meaning it. In this loose sense, world includes other minds, that kind of mathematics which suspends any exercise of belief in bodies, and God (III 121, 31 through 122, 6).

But suspension of exercise of belief in world, even in the loose sense of "world," still leaves three transcendences, in the loose sense (III 140, 11–20):

(1) The transcendence of reflection (IX 171–80; XI 204–5, 11): an act (or a state of sensibility) in the time-stream (the stream which is the form of flowing acts or states) insofar as that act (or state) stands over against other acts in the same time-stream, other acts which mean and manifest the first act (or state). The many and different acts reflecting on and the act (or state) reflected on again and again as one and the same act (or state) are both within one and the same time-stream. The reflecting and the reflected-on are each in the horizon of the other, the reflecting in the protentional horizon of the reflected-on and the reflected-on in the retentional horizon of the reflecting.

(2) The pure I (*Vollzugs- und Deckungsich*), free of apperceptions of *Realität* (*Träger von Eigenschaften; Zustände abhängig von Umständen*), is transcendent over against its acts (III 137–38, esp. 138, 17–19; IV 101–4, esp. 102, 37 through 103, 12; XIV 29, 30–31).

(3) The transcendence of the time-stream (less exactly so-called) and of all that which is in the time-stream over against the pretemporal form of temporality which forms the time-stream: "Die starre Form der lebendigen Gegenwart (der vollen 'Gegenwart') und das diese Form Durchströmende: eine Zeitlosigkeit der Form, in der Zeit sich konstituiert" (XI 392, 13–15).

The stream of presencings is *irreeller Erwerb* of the *Ur-Ich*.[2]

---

2. MS C 2 I. Differences after the transcendental reduction:
The distinction between the stream of presencings itself (less exactly called the time-stream) and all that which is present in the stream clarifies the distance and the bridging of distance found even when the presenced (that-which-is-present) in the stream has not yet been modified into that which is present only through the presencing of the absenced presencing of it: through retention. Presencing overcomes in the unity of "intentional immanence" two different kinds of "*reell* transcendence" or difference: the

Husserlian Distinctions and Strategies   53

For Husserl there are two reservations on the primacy of presence, two limits to the principle *manifestandum est*:

(1) Presencing distended, the timeless form of temporality, is the last form of constitution, the frame of sense-formation. (The task of reason is meaningful, even though it can never be so completed that its sense is filled by an achievement with nothing left still to be achieved.)

(2) Complication and reversal of presence and absence is the form of the community of monads, the unity of a plurality of irreducibly different perspectives: the other is presenced as an absent presencing. So the *solus ipse* through reflection on its own othering of itself (my own past is both mine and alien: *ego* declines itself into *me*) quiets its fear of losing the *alter ego: te*.[3] But the other is for me a presenced absent presencing such that to strike out "absent" neither ever can have made sense nor ever will make sense.

Yet given that the alien and absence and sense cannot be converted without context and remainder into my own and presence and achieve-

---

difference between the achieving presencing (the not-yet-absenced presencing) and the elapsed presencing (the absenced presencing) and the difference between the achieving presencing (which also presences the elapsed presencing as part of the stream itself) and that which the achieving presencing presences in the stream, that which is present in the stream (not part of the stream of presencings itself). Husserl's terms: the stream of presencings itself: *Längsintentionalität*; that which is present in the stream of presencings: *Querintentionalität*.

The achieving presencing achieves the perspectival orientation of elapsed (and anticipated) presencings around its achievement of states of sensibility and acts of interpretation and reflection. "And the achieving presencing presences itself to itself ?" No, here there is no absencing to be overcome in presencing, no difference to be overcome in unity, no distance to be bridged, but rather the primordial occasion, not the occasionality of an act in the stream, not *cogito*, but *fungor* with a double achievement, the presencing of the stream of presencings and the presencing of that which is present in the stream, not a third achievement ("the presencing by the achieving presencing of itself to itself "), but only the achieving of the two achievements.

All this can be meant and manifested by acts in the stream (such *cogitationes* are the acme of the phenomenology of phenomenology), but then the *fungor* is not meant and manifested as an act.

The invariant across the difference between the achieving presencing and the elapsed (and anticipated) presencings is an *eidos* which can be meant and manifested by acts in the stream, but this *eidos* (primordial occasionality) is not the *fungor*, the primordial occasion.

The scare quotes ("intentional immanence" and "*reell* transcendence") are an index of denomination from the weaker; see X 75, 12–22; 283, 26 through 284, 6; III 206, 16 through 207, 12; *Logische Untersuchungen* I ("Ausdruck und Bedeutung") no. 10 *in fine*; *Erfahrung und Urteil* no. 23 (a) *ad finem*.

3. I 144, 38 through 145, 24; 155, 7ff.; 161, 11–38; VI 175, 17–36; 188, 31 through 189, 31; VII 264, 38 through 265, 37; VIII 62, 28 through 63, 7; 134–37; 174–76; 188–90; 436 note; IX 456, 6–8; 536 note.

ment, nevertheless there is a teleology toward appropriation and manifestation and completion.

Husserl exploits two conflicts in order to generate and legitimate the sense of transcendental phenomenology (transcendental phenomenology is the sense confusedly and obscurely anticipated in the originating sense of philosophy):

(1) The conflict between an originating sense and a derivative sense, which nevertheless presupposes and uses the originating sense. The derivative sense either ignores or misunderstands or denies and thus in any case conceals its own origin.

(a) Greek philosophy achieved the sense of the science of *hen panta* only within the horizon of the transcendent world and the world-transcendent.

(b) Modern philosophy understood the sense of transcendental, non-worldly world-constituting subjectivity only as still confused with subjectivity at work within the already constituted world.

(c) The mathematical science of nature either (i) tried to achieve the sense of the universality of science by ingesting—or at least by serving as a model for—both the science of mind and the science of the prescientific world or (ii) it left mind and the prescientific world out and thus gave up the sense of universality.

(2) The conflict between science and the scientist practicing science in the context of the prescientific world and between the prescientific world, which is a condition for science, and the world as it is for science. Science attempts to encompass its prescientific condition and therefore also the scientist, who practices science in the context of the prescientific world. On the other hand, the prescientific world encompasses the scientist and his activity, science. Either science is a worldview among others or there is a science of world-views.

Mind as science and the science of mind are in conflict: originating and derivative, sensed and achieved, encompassing and encompassed. Only transcendental phenomenology as the non-worldly science of non-worldly world-constituting subjectivity can resolve these conflicts.

Science would seem to have either to take for granted the prescientific world (and thus to give up the sense of science as having a universal theme and method) or to convert the prescientific world into a theme for scientific method. This issue is transposed into the issue of scientist and science insofar as the scientist practices science in the context of the prescientific. If there is no science of this context and of the practice of science, science is built on unscientific foundations: *pudenda origo*.

Here Husserl moves to establish the sense of a science that is phenomenological but not transcendental, rigorous but not mathematical, a science whose theme is the prescientific world, both predicative and prepredicative, both traditional and thingly. Called a science insofar as it follows the web of apperceptions, thematizing in evidence the invariant within free variation, it is phenomenological because its theme is manifested meaning-acts through which alone the world meant in these meaning-acts is constituted. But this science is not the full and final sense of science because its theme is only the prescientific world and thus not universal. It does not suspend all exercise of belief in world, and thus it tries to carry out from within the believed-in world the analysis of the constitution of world.

"... [D]ie thematische Ausschließung besagt nicht das Außer-Geltungsetzen ..." (IX 232, 37–38):[4] this distinguishes the sciences of nature and the *Geisteswissenschaften* from each other and from transcendental phenomenology. For the sciences of nature the meaning-acts of the scientist—both practicing science and living in the prescientific context of science—are unthematic but operative. For the *Geisteswissenschaften* bodies are unthematic, but belief in bodies is operative and thematic as well insofar as body is (1) the center of orientation of the appearings of bodies and (2) both the expression and a theme of meaning-acts. The unthematic meaning-acts operative in the sciences of nature and the belief in bodies operative in the *Geisteswissenschaften* are not operative as acts of transcendental phenomenology, but both are themes for transcendental phenomenology.

In the posttranscendental attitude, the no longer anonymous transcendental is unthematic, but there is an apperception of the already achieved reduction, the accent in the sense of reduction having shifted from suspension of exercise of belief in the world to thematization of the at first anonymous constitution of that belief.

Science in the pretranscendental attitude either gives up its claim to universality or assimilates its non-scientific context and itself as an activity to the mathematical science of nature as a system of bodies, in the extreme excluding as a theme the specificity of besouledness (*Leib*). (This extreme bleaches out for the community of science those uniquely oriented appearings of bodies which are nevertheless a pre-

---

4. III 118–21; IV 174; 179–80; 286–88; 369, 38 through 370, 14; VI 308, 32 through 309, 8; 398–401, esp. 400, 18 & 28–29; VIII 139–45; 447, 35–47; 450, 10–22; 455, 13–21, 34–47; 457, 5–39; IX 147–50; 230, 21 through 233, 29. Within the transcendental epoché there is a thematic epoché of others which *considers* only one's own transcendentality but leaves transcendental *belief* in transcendental others untouched.

supposition of the constructing and substructing mathematicization of those appearings.) *Geisteswissenschaft,* which resists this assimilation, would seem to avoid these alternatives, but taking the universal system of meaning-acts, and especially the system of acts meaning the prescientific world, as its theme, it nevertheless apperceives bodies as a presupposition (as *fundierend*) and does not thematize the non-worldly constitution or sense-formation of the horizon "world." Only the non-worldly science of non-worldly world-constitution can resolve these dilemmas by outflanking both the prescientific world-horizon and science as an activity within that horizon and by thematizing belief in bodies without any apperception of believed-in bodies, but this science must thematize its self-diremption, its return to the natural attitude, a return which is the condition of its accessibility within the world: the rhetoric of transcendental speech: "Wie die Phänomenologie alles Nichtphänomenologische in Form der 'Einklammerung' umspannt, so auch das, was gegebenenfalls Überschreitung einer phänomenologischen Betrachtung heißt: alle Rechtfertigungen aber gehören nach Sinn und möglicher Geltung in die Phänomenologie, also auch die der betreffenden Arten von Überschreitungen" (V 89, 21–27; VII 85, 30; VIII 76, 17 through 78, 26; 82–83; 179, 30–35; 180, 22–25; 182, 15–16; IX 294, 13–26; 343, 10–11; 614, ad 295, 9; XIII 200–211, esp. 208).

The prescientific world encompassing science is subjective in the sense that all is relative to one among many other and different ones. This is a confused and obscure indication that the full and final sense of science must be subjective if it is to be universal—but subjective in a transcendental, not in a mundane way. The failure of mundane subjectivity to be universal (because all is relative to merely one among many other and different ones: *Endchen der Welt, Weltstück*) (VII 339, 30–46) is a mirror-image of the failure of mundane science to reflect radically on its own subjectivity. The mundane subjective and the mundane scientific try to ingest each other, but each is recalcitrant to the other's claim. Mundane science makes a claim to universality which it cannot make good because it cannot include the subjective in a non-scientific mode, a mode which continues to revive against the claim of mundane science to have included it. On the other hand, mundane subjectivity makes its own claim to universality ("all is relative to one"), but this claim cannot be made good because the one is merely one among many other and different ones. Only with the shift from mundane subjectivity to transcendental subjectivity can subjectivity make good a claim to universality (including constitution of the open community of other I's), just as only with the shift from mundane science to transcendental science can science make good a claim to include its own subjectivity within its theme.

(1) The shift of interest from what is manifested to the modes of its manifestness and to the acts which manifest it, and from themes within the horizon "world" (a web of silent, dark, and unquestioned beliefs) to that horizon itself as articulated and clarified theme, and then to the process which accomplishes that web of beliefs; (2) the dative of manifestation (manifesting is manifesting *to*)—taking these two [(1) & (2)] together cantilevers us toward non-worldly world-constituting subjectivity as a theme.

The Crisis does little toward achieving the task of transcendental phenomenology, the science of non-worldly world-constituting subjectivity. It is rather a protreptic toward the legitimacy and the necessity of the sense of that task, a rhetoric using as available means of persuasion the paradoxes and antagonisms that result from trying to achieve the sense of the science of *hen panta* without distinguishing the subjectivity that constitutes the world from the subjectivity that works within the constituted world. The crisis in the vocation to achieve the sense of the science of *hen panta* is a crisis of responsibility because that sense can be achieved only by one to whom that science is manifest. The crisis can be resolved only by a shift in the sense of this dative of manifestation. But the responsible one to *whom* ("dative") the way to achieving the sense of the science of *hen panta* is manifest and the one *who* ("nominative") speaks of that way to achieving that sense is also for us (who read the residue in the world of the speech of Husserl as transcendental I) one who is manifest*ed* (as a transcendence: "accusative"), and there are many manifestings *of* ("genitive") that one manifested to us who are in the world. The synthesis of the new, transcendental sense of the dative and the nominative with the old, mundane ("natural") sense of the accusative and the genitive is still a question.

What is the chance, the violence, or the grace through which each of us might make his own Husserl's words (the words of one who worked among us in our world) in which he writes of himself as using in a new sense the word *I*?

"Kann ich die phänomenologische Reduktion eines anderen Menschen verstehen, ohne selbst phänomenologische Reduktion zu üben oder mindestens in eine Motivation hineinzugeraten, in der sie mir sich aufnötigt—... Kann für mich also in der Welt eine phänomenologische Reduktion vorkommen, ohne daß ich selbst sie wirklich geübt hätte?" (XV 537, 5–13).

10

Quotation and Writing, Egos and Tokenings, Variables and Gaps

I use a language in speaking a speech in the sense of forming a sentence. A speech so spoken is sometimes also not only formed (used`) by me but also appropriated (used′), and as appropriated it is a statement made, not just a sentence formed, by me. Sometimes a sentence formed by me is not spoken as a statement made by me; rather it is quoted, spoken by me as a statement made by another speaker or as having been, but no longer being, a statement made by me.

Sometimes I speak and use′ as my own a speech in order to mention a speech which I or another speaker spoke and used′ and which I or another speaker will speak and use′. The mediation of such use′/mention/use′ to each other by writing is a sense in which we can use′ and not only mention the phrase *the ideality of meaning*.

Saying the same, the same remaining invariant across differing sayings, makes writing possible. Detachment and distancing of a speech from this speaker speaking now is the condition of its availability as the same speech again and again and for others. If a speech could not be detached and distanced from speaker and speaking, then the difference between speakers and between speech acts would make impossible both quotation and appropriation of a speech as the same speech but spoken by different speakers or by the same speaker again. Sometimes a speaker is able to quote and sometimes also to appropriate his own past speech or the speech of another speaker. Both quotation and appropriation of a speech are acts of repetition of a speech as the same but with reference to another, originating speech act or also to another, originating speaker. In anticipation of repetition of a speech as the same but spoken in another speech act or also by another speaker, we detach speech from the ephemerality of this speaker speaking now: *Aufhebung* of absence (*lēthē*) by detachment.

Not the only but the clearest form of this detachment is writing.

When we quote or appropriate, rather than originate, a speech as the same speech spoken again in another speech act or also by another speaker, we recapitulate the anticipation of this repetition and the consequence of this anticipation: the detachment which is the condition of repetition. We take together both the derivativeness of the speech as quoted or appropriated and the impossibility of a repetition of the originating speech act: the originating speech act and the detachment of the speech from that speech act; repetition of the speech; sedimentation of the attachment of the speech to the originating speech act; thematization of the speech as repeated; thematization of the originating but irrepeatable speech act as horizon of the repeated speech.

Writing is the clearest form of that detachment which makes a speech available again and again as the same, holding out invariant against modifications—against the difference between speech acts and between speakers and against the difference between presence and absence of what is spoken about.

Sometimes I speak and use´ as my own a speech in order to mention a used´ speech which I not only did not but could not and not only will not but will not be able to speak and use´. Sometimes there is quotation (not only replication of the texture of tokens or of the sign designs) of a speech without the possibility of appropriation of that speech by the quoting speaker.

The mediation of such use´/mention/use´ to each other by one I-as-speaker is a sense (sense$_1$) in which we can only mention but not use´ the phrase *the transcendental ego*.

Transcendental ego$_1$, so to speak, tokens the tokens of both the speech first used´ and the speech then used´ to mention the speech first used´ and in so tokening he speaks and uses´ each and both of these speeches together as his own and in his own right. Either transcendental ego$_1$ can token, or he cannot; if he cannot, then we cannot hear what he has to say; on the other hand, if he says anything, he appropriates two speeches, only one of which a transcendentally anonymous and naive speaker can speak as his own and in his own right, the other of which the same transcendentally anonymous and naive speaker can only mention but cannot use´. Transcendental ego$_1$ appropriates both speeches together, only one of which can be used´ and the other of which can only be mentioned by any tokening speaker. We must, it seems, accept either a nontokening speaker or a collection of speeches which as a collection is free-floating: unused´ and unowned by one speaker and, because unused´ and unowned, unaddressed.

Transcendental ego$_1$ is the confusion that results from appropriation to one speaker of the collection of all the tokens of the severally spoken and used´ speeches and from consideration of all these tokens as tokens of the used´ speech of one speaker. When it is objected that it is impossible for such a collection of tokens to be considered as tokens of the appropriated speech of one speaker, as tokens produced by the tokenings of an appropriating speaker, then it is answered that the speech of that speaker cannot be tokened. But no sense of *I* can be incompatible with, although perhaps some sense of *I* is irreducible to, this sense: the tokener tokening a member of the token-class *I* in the language I am using, or whatever sign design plays the same role in any other language: a design as a member of a token-class whose members are produced in order to designate only the producer as a speaker, as using, in the act of producing the token, a language.

One-to-one correlation of transcendentally anonymous and naive speakers with transcendental egos suggests that the mapping of transcendentally anonymous and naive speakers into transcendental egos is otiose. A nonotiose mapping would be many-to-one and such a mapping would require either that transcendental ego$_1$ use´ incompatible tokening-reflexives or that he not token at all in speaking.

Compare this caricature of the transcendental ego as ventriloquist to playing a recording of the speech of two speakers, the speech of each of whom contains the tokening-reflexive *I*, and to taking the played recording as the appropriated speech of one speaker. (The tokens of the live speeches and of the playback are not the same, although they are members of the same token-classes.) Such recording-and-playback is detachment of speech from speech act and speaker, but a detachment that tends to obscure itself in a way writing does not. (Is there a distinction in speech comparable to the distinction in writing between handwriting and printing?)

We have supposed, and reduced to absurdity, that the constitution of human speeches in the world implies the use´ of all such speeches by one transcendental ego, a nonhuman and nonworldly speaker: transcendental ego$_1$ is a *hinterweltlicher* ventriloquist constituting human and worldly speeches by using´ them.

Suppose that human and worldly speeches are spoken by being mentioned by an I-as-speaker (transcendental ego$_2$) who can use´ no worldly speech because such use´ would imply the mundification of the speaker and therefore the loss of his status as nonworldly speaker of worldly speeches as worldly and therefore also as nonworldly speaker of world as world. But such a speaker cannot use´ the worldly speech "I can only mention and can never use´ worldly speeches." On the other hand, were he to say the same in transcendentalese, were he to translate that speech in mundanese into transcendentalese, then no transcendentally anonymous and naive, human and worldly speaker could understand him. The speaker cannot say to the hearer in the hearer's language "I only mention speeches in your language" because he would be using´ that speech in the hearer's language (in mundanese: transcendentally anonymous and naive, human and worldly language); his denial of mundane use´ would be a mundanely used´ speech. If the speaker can only mention speeches in the hearer's language, how can he teach users of that language to use his own language (transcendentalese)?

If the transcendental acts that thematize human and worldly speeches as human and worldly are nonhuman and nonworldly acts of a speaker who is therefore nonhuman and nonworldly (but not *hinterweltlich*), and if such transcendental speech acts can be neither only use´ nor only mention of transcendentally anonymous and naive, human and worldly speeches, then perhaps transcendental thematization of such speeches as human and worldly is use´ of some such speeches and mention only of other such speeches. But either the use´ of any unreduced speech by the transcendental I-as-speaker would taint his transcendental purity with a tag-end of mundification or such use´ would make the distinction between the transcendental and the mundane otiose.

Nor can the transcendentally anonymous and naive, human and worldly speaker learn to use transcendentalese in whatever way or ways the child learns to use his first language. Transcendentalese constitutes mundanese by setting itself up in contrasting difference from mundanese (this differentiation consists in thematizing world as world: presencing the presence/absence of that-which-is-present/absent). As constitutive of mundanese by contrast, transcendentalese is nevertheless also a translation from and a quotation of mundanese and is in this sense parasitic on already used´ speeches in an already used language.

Perhaps the grafting or staggering or imbrication of systems can give another sense (sense$_3$) to the transcendental ego:

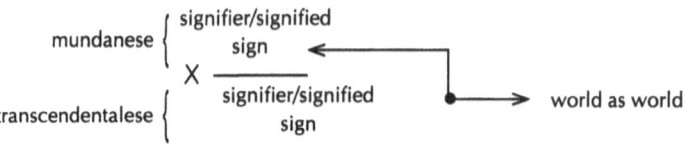

× is (1) a sign used′ by a transcendentally anonymous and naive, human and worldly speaker as a sign in mundanese; and (2) a sign used` as a signifier by a transcendental I-as-speaker (transcendental ego in sense₃) in a used′ sign in transcendentalese; and (3): (1) signified and mentioned, bracketed, quoted but not appropriated (used′) by the speaker (user′) of a speech (sign) in transcendentalese. (World signified as world is world thematized.)

A collection of speeches spoken and used′ out of a language matrix becomes itself a new language matrix to be used to speak and use′ another speech; a speech (used′ sign) mentions (signifies) other speeches (used′ signs), forming (using`) them as signifiers in the language in which it is spoken and used′; a speech both steals and returns other speeches, disappropriating them by using` them as signifiers, but also restoring them to their first use′ as signs.

The transcendental reduction[1] steals mundane, transcendentally anonymous and naive, human and worldly speeches, uses` them as signifiers in transcendentalese to mention (signify) them as mundanely used′ speeches, and then returns them ("the apperception of the natural attitude") to their mundane use′ as signs.

If we try to hold a first-order speech down to being only a sign, it slips away and turns up elsewhere, *in* a second-order speech, as a signifier; if we try to hold the signifier in a second-order speech down to being only a signifier, it slips away and turns up elsewhere, *as* a first-order speech, as a sign. This alibi structure of $\frac{\text{sign}}{\text{signifer}}$ accounts for the irreducible ambiguity of mundane/transcendental. A sign in mundanese can be also elsewhere, as a signifier in transcendentalese; a signifier in transcendentalese is always also elsewhere, as a sign in mundanese. Transcendentally reduced speech uses` as a signifier what it mentions (signifies) in a used′ speech in transcendentalese as being used′ as a sign in mundanese.

The signified of transcendental speech (of transcendentally used′

---

1. Reduction can be considered as a device (*priyom*) for defamiliarizing speeches, both by speaking about the language in which a speech is spoken, resolving the speech back into its language, and by making of already spoken speeches a new language in which to speak a new speech. This defamiliarization is in the service of clarification of mundane clarifications as such, as mundane and as clarifications.

signs) is the signifier of the same speech but signified as mundane speech (as mundanely used´ signs with their mundane signifiers and signifieds). This reflexivity is an affinity between the transcendental and the grammatical: "This sentence is in correct English." is a sign signifying its signifier as well-formed.

The signified of transcendental speech includes the theme "world": its own signifiers thematized as worldly speech (as mundanely used´ signs). Transcendental speech (transcendentally used´ signs) signifying world as world is not *as the unity of signifier/signified* itself worldly, although it uses` worldly speeches (what other language could it use?)—but as signifiers, not as signs; the difference is thematization of world. Transcendental signification uses` mundane signification, not as signification, but rather as signifier; transcendental signification uses` its signifiers to mention (signify) them as thematically mundane significations (mundane signs used´ mundanely).

But what are the presuppositions motivating the position or thesis that world can be thematized? *Meletē thanatou: Sein zum Tode.*

Mapped onto each other are states-of-affairs considered not as stated but as structures and structures considered not as statements but as structures usable or used, on condition of this mapping, for stating states-of-affairs.

To what extent are rules for constructing such structures (structures usable or used for stating states-of-affairs) by relating elements and structures of elements, rules statable without stating that such structures are usable or used for stating states-of-affairs?

A structure appropriated as a statement is more than the structure of the statement, and a stated state-of-affairs is more than the structure that comes to be stated.

"———" is true: ———.
mentioned,   used,
not used,   not mentioned,
but usable   but mentionable

Such quotation exhibits a structure as unappropriated and thus calls attention to the difference between the structure appropriated and the appropriation of the structure. More exactly: let two forms of quotation differentiate what is at work in a statement without being the statement as true: the spoken or written string (texture of tokens; sign designs) and whatever is more than the string but less than the statement as true: *———* means †———†, which is true.

Were there no speaker distinct from a system of possibilities of speech, no speaker as principle of choice between the mutually exclusive speeches virtual in the language system, then either the system of possibilities of speech would be reduced to mutually exclusive speeches, or there would be no speeches at all but only the system of possibilities of speech. There could not be only language; language dirempts into, without being exhausted by, speeches. In order that there be speeches and not just the system of possibilities of speech, there must be a principle of choice from the matrix of the language system, and neither language nor speeches can choose because language is only the system of possibilities of mutually exclusive speeches, and speeches are already chosen.

But we must not confuse speeches as sentences formed (use`) and speeches as statements made (use´). Sentences may be well-formed by a blind calculus and then become statements made by a speaker: free-floating sentences are appropriated and thus become stated sentences or statements made; statements made or stated sentences are detached and thus become free-floating sentences.

The tacitness which is the irreducibility of a language to sentences is not the elusiveness of *I*, insofar as *I* is the maker of statements, and not only the former of sentences. What is the difference between forming sentences and making statements? Appropriation: but what is the *proprium* implied by appropriation *to* and detachment *from*? That which is referred to as being of such a kind as to form sentences? No, or not only.

Sometimes I speak so that I can hear myself speaking as if another were speaking too or instead; sometimes another speaks so that I can hear him speaking as if I myself were speaking too or instead. How do shifters break this indifference?

The teleology of language as presencing: an anticipated implosion of speakers, chain, choice: appropriation of all quotations, contraction of the speech flow, exhaustion of the language matrix and thus performance of mutually exclusive speeches; negativity exploding this anticipated presence-without-absence back again into the plurality of quoted speakers, the distention of syntagms, the virtuality of paradigms.

Schemata, stencils or frames, forms, not names; gaps in patterns (gaps indicated by indicators which also indicate restrictions on filling), not variables; differential chain and choice (division and combination, deletion and substitution): the outflanking of *logos* as the interplay of *noein* and *einai*: not speech as collecting out of hiddenness and absence into manifestness and presence, but emptiness: not the emptiness of the unsaturated which is to be saturated, not the signified absence of a named, not the signifying absence of any name,[2] not even the differentiation of presence and absence, which keeps open the space of their interplay; not absence, difference from presence in the order of presence, and not the space of the interplay of presence and absence as different; but "~~emptiness~~" (see Scholium II).

It is within this emptiness that a speech is born and anticipates its death: no longer to be used´ but only to be mentioned.

It is within this emptiness that a language is born and anticipates its death: no longer to be used but only to be mentioned.

But to mention this speech and this language is to use´ a speech and to use a language.

SCHOLIUM

... let appearings themselves appear in a style of appearing proper to them. Appearings themselves can appear (as that which appears and not as appearings of that which appears) only in contrast with a background: themselves as the appearings of that which appears preveniently. We have staggered systems:

$$\begin{array}{c} \text{mundane} \\ \text{that which appears / \underline{its appearings}} \\ \text{that which appears / its appearings} \\ \text{transcendental} \end{array}$$

$$\frac{A/\underline{B}}{a/b}$$

The *Endchen der Welt* difficulty can be formulated as the tendency to assimilate a/b to A/B. The *nulla re indiget* difficulty can be formulated as the tendency to separate a/b from A/B.

$\frac{A/B}{a/b}$ itself is that which appears to "first philosophy":

$$\frac{A/B}{a/b} \Big/ \beta$$

---

2. A sign of the pervasiveness of the teleology of presencing: the very absence of a signifier can be used as signifier of whatever is signified (and thus presenced-in-absence).

11
The Logic of Modernity

Professor Galgan has written a history of modern philosophy.[1] His specific intent and achievement is the telling of a story, a story about that period or epoch of philosophy which defines itself by both following on and setting itself against both ancient philosophy and medieval philosophy (and theology). Philosophy becomes ancient or old only when there is a sense of newness which sets itself up in difference to what until then was simply philosophy, philosophy *tout court*, not ancient or old philosophy. And in turn when philosophy sets itself up as new in difference to that first newness, we call the newly new philosophy modern; and the old new philosophy, the philosophy between the old and the newly new, we call the in-between philosophy or middle philosophy or medieval philosophy (and theology).

Professor Galgan tells a story. A story in relation to whatever it is a story about, a story in relation to its world, does two things: first, it selects; it limits and trims by selecting; second, it organizes, it tightens the relations among the elements it selects. As Aristotle says in talking about the plot and the action the plot imitates, the plot has a beginning and an end and the elements in the plot follow one another with a degree of necessity lacking in the action itself. The plot therefore contrasts both with everything that happened and with one thing happening merely after another and not because of another.

I wish to raise several questions about Professor Galgan's book by raising questions, first, about what went before the beginning and what comes after the end of the story he tells and, second, about the principles he uses to organize or to pattern the events or moments in "the logic of modernity" his story displays.

Third, I wish to ask to what extent the point of view from which Professor Galgan tells the story is identified with the points of view

---

[1]. A review of Gerald J. Galgan, *The Logic of Modernity* (New York: New York University Press, 1982).

he tells about in the story and to what extent Professor Galgan, as teller of the story, takes a different point of view over against the points of view he tells about in the story.

The story introduces artificial cuts which, by dividing from what went before and from what comes after, make a beginning and an end. Consider a bit of dialogue from Mozart's *The Magic Flute:*

> PAMINA: So you know my good and gentle mother?
> PAPAGENO: If you are the daughter of the Queen of the Night, yes.
> PAMINA: Oh, I am!
> PAPAGENO: I shall soon see by comparing you with this picture.
> Eyes brown: yes, brown.
> Lips red: yes, red.
> Hair blond: yes, blond.
> Everything fits, except the hands and feet. According to this painting you shouldn't have any hands or feet.

Although the representation does not represent the hands and feet of the lady, we know that the represented lady nevertheless has hands and feet. Even though a story makes cuts in the action by beginning and ending, the story will not abstain completely from telling about what went before the beginning and what comes after the end; there will be spillover. I wish to raise questions about the Greek philosophy and the Christian theology which precede the beginning of Professor Galgan's story but which nevertheless get into that story in a very important way. And I wish to raise a question about what follows the end of the story but nevertheless gets into the story.

Briefly, those questions are these: First, is the view of Greek philosophy *truncated*? In discussing this question I wish to recall Epicurus. Second, is the view of Christian theological doctrines *distorted*? In discussing this question I wish to recall orthodox doctrines of the Trinity, creation, and the Incarnation. Third, is the view of post-modern philosophy-*cum*-theology merely *conjectural*, that is, is the anticipation of a "rough beast, its hour come at last, slouching towards Bethlehem to be born" a mere conjecture based on the truncation of Greek philosophy and the distortion of Christian theology? In discussing this question I wish to recall Heidegger. To recapitulate: against truncation, Epicurus; against distortion, orthodox theology of the Trinity, creation, and the Incarnation; against mere conjecture based on truncation and distortion, Heidegger.

Before I make these three points, let me go back to the tightening of the relations among the elements in the story. It seems to me that Professor Galgan tells the story of modernity by means of the organizing principle of unmasking. Masking implies a duality that hides itself by presenting itself as a unity. In Professor Galgan's terms: first, the claim to know the natural is unmasked as hiding the gap between inner and outer; second, ideological superstructure hides philosophical substructure and philosophical substructure hides ideological superstructure; looking at either one, we unmask when we see the other one, at first sight hidden; third, inheritance or tradition is both accepted and rejected; it is rejected, but that rejection is unmasked as being fed by a continuing, subterranean acceptance; and it is accepted, but that acceptance is unmasked as being a distortion of the original, and that distortion is a kind of rejection.

This brings us back to the issue of Greek philosophy and Christian theology. Professor Galgan's book begins by speaking of "the ancient 'mythos'" and "the medieval 'mythos.'" Greek philosophy simply or *tout court* is presented as teaching a finite cosmos of necessary and eternal kinds with chance and choice confined to the sublunary center and man finding his happiness in contemplation of kinds and of contemplation itself. But Greek is not only Aristotelian. Epicurus, for instance, is Greek, but he teaches infinite atoms and void without heterogeneity and hierarchy of obvious kinds, the chance origin of cosmos and kinds, and happiness in the well-being of noncontemplative pleasure.

After Greek philosophy, what of Christian theology?

In orthodox theology of the Trinity the procession of the Son or Word from the Father and of the Spirit from the Father and the Son or Word is not a loss recouped by a return to the origin enriched by the inclusion of the recouped loss; Hegel to the contrary, *Aufhebung* or uplift to the contrary, otherness is not necessarily loss or contradiction.

In orthodox theology of creation the plenitude of God is not filled out, not enriched or augmented or complemented by creatures or by the creating of creatures; nor does the Creator lose or contradict Himself in the being of creatures or in letting be the being of creatures. Because creatures are other than God, it does not follow that they are God othering Himself.

In orthodox theology of the Incarnation, there is no blending or merging or confusion of divinity with humanity; Christ is not like the teacher of Achilles, Chiron, the centaur, half man and therefore not wholly human, half horse and therefore not wholly equine; Christ is wholly divine, wholly human, not in a confusion of two natures but in the oneness of person of the Son, other to the Father without loss or contradiction, the Word in whom creatures are created without loss or contradiction and redeemed without blending or merging or confusion of divine with human.

And what comes after the end?

Heidegger has given us a reading of Greek philosophy, of the corewords of Greek philosophy: *logos* or word, *physis* or nature, *nous* or mind, *ousia* or being, *doxa* or display, a reading that is not only Aristotelian; and he has given us a reading of world-technology which sees its roots not in secularized Christian theology but in implications of Greek philosophy itself. Heidegger is post-modern; he comes after the end of Professor Galgan's story. At the end of his story, Professor Galgan conjectures about what seems to me to be a new revelation or unmasking which would throw off sacramental hiddenness. I do not know whether Professor Galgan speaks here in his own voice or whether he speaks from the point of view of the Hegelian, who, as the completion of modernity, also speaks of what comes after the end. Perhaps for Professor Galgan his own voice and the voice of the end of modernity speaking of what is on the other side of the cut which marks the end of modernity are one and the same voice.

For myself, I prefer to join what is after the end with what is before the beginning. Heidegger has taught us an interplay of hiddenness and manifestation which is beyond the dialectic or push-pull of inner and outer, beyond the dialectic or push-pull of ideological superstructure and philosophical substructure, beyond the dialectic or push-pull of acceptance and rejection of inheritance or tradition: he has taught us that the otherness of hiddenness and truth to each other is not an otherness of loss or contradiction: they rest in each other; they are not violently wrested from each other. Perhaps Heidegger indicates a way[2] both to a rediscovery of Greek philosophy and to a rediscovery of Christian theology, to a rediscovery of what has been before the beginning and will be after the end of modernity, whose story Professor Galgan tells so well.

I would like to end with some remarks about a formulation at the end of Professor Galgan's book. He speaks of the coming into unhiddenness of the hidden condition of technology, a coming into unhiddenness which intimates the possibility of a new presencing of God and which opens the possibility of prayer to a more-than-natural divine (pp. 397–98).

The word "nature" means, among other ways, by way of contrast, or at least of difference, to what is in our power to bring to be by

---

2. Heidegger opens up a space beyond the dialectic or push-pull between parts and whole and between obscurity and clarity. This space is not theologized; precisely therein lies its importance for theology. Aquinas used Aristotle's nontheologized understanding of the self-sufficiency and necessity and intelligibility of *natures* as an index of the self-sufficiency and necessity and intelligibility of the divine *nature*, the self-sufficiency and necessity and intelligibility, which are for Aquinas the roots of the divine freedom to choose to create or not to create and to choose *what* to create.

choice and construction. Technology has shifted the place where the dividing line that marks the difference is drawn, but it has not done away with the difference itself. (Not even Nietzsche makes sense of doing away with the difference between nature and power.) Now if by "a more-than-natural divine" we mean the freedom-to-choose and the power-to-make of the infinite God, creator of created natures, we should not forget that the meaning of "natural" in the phrase "more-than-natural" is embedded in a deeper or overarching sense of "nature"—the nature that is God Himself, who is not created, not subject to freedom and power, neither to His own nor to ours. Uncreated nature, as eternity and necessity, as self-sufficiency and intelligibility, suffuses the generosity and the power in the light of which created natures are conditioned and therefore can appear to us as malleable by our power.

The "logic of modernity" can try to throw out the nature of Greek philosophy and the uncreated nature and the created natures of Christian theology, but nature will nevertheless come back. Indeed, it will never have been thrown out, except for a logic which, like the *logos* of the opponent in Aristotle's *Metaphysics* IV 4, has undermined its own conditions.

A giver who lacks self-sufficiency and therefore gains for himself and thus changes by giving a gift to another does not give with a generosity unmixed with something other than generosity, namely, a change toward self-completion. And because a gift is given freely and not necessarily, it does not follow that the giving is infected with absurdity.

Just as for Aristotle the self-destruction of the opponent's *logos* manifests the self-manifestation (*doxa*) of the necessity of the true *logos* (the self-manifestation of this necessity is not wrested from the self-destruction of the opponent's *logos*), so the self-destruction of Hegel's *logos*, the culmination of "the logic of modernity," manifests the self-manifestation of the plenitude of the *logos* of Christian theology (the self-manifestation of this plenitude is not wrested from the self-destruction of Hegel's *logos*). Although the corruption of the best is worst, the false can always become the occasion for manifesting the self-manifestation of the true, which in its necessity and plenitude shows up the false as false, indeed as self-destructive. But the false and indeed self-destructive *logos* is not that obscurity out of which the true *logos* is manifest and in which it rests.

This, I think, is what Professor Galgan's book shows.

SUMMARY

The articulation of the history of philosophy into epochs (ancient, medieval, modern, post-modern) on the basis of shifts in the senses of "nature"; admiration of excellence, praise of self-sufficiency and gratitude toward generosity, pride in mastery; the interplay of tradition and novelty; a common generalization about "ancient" philosophy falsified by Epicureanism; Hegelian distortions of theological themes: Trinity, creation, Incarnation; Heidegger's recapitulation of crucial Greek themes: *logos, physis, ousia, nous, doxa*; Heidegger's non-Hegelian understanding of the interplay of hiddenness and manifestation; the contrast between the role of contradiction in Hegelian *logos* and in Aristotelian *logos, Metaphysics* IV 4.

12

Husserl, Heidegger, Early and Late, and Aquinas

PREFACE

This lecture is about some relationships among several themes in Heidegger's early course lectures given in Marburg in the Winter Semester of 1925/6 and in the Summer Semester of 1927, in *Being and Time,* which was published in 1927, and in his later development. That later development can be fairly represented by his last two sets of course lectures, given in Freiburg in the Summer Semesters of 1943 and 1944 on Heraclitus; by his last public lecture, called "Time and Being," given in 1962; by a seminar on that lecture, also in 1962; and by four further seminars, held in 1966, 1968, 1969, and 1973. Heidegger died in 1976 at the age of eighty-six.

My lecture today suffers from two kinds of zig-zag. Ideally an understanding of the several themes themselves would be assumed, permitting the exposition to focus on the relationships among them. But in fact, considering the occasion, the lecture has to zig-zag back and forth between a summary exposition of the themes themselves and a summary exposition of the relationships among them. That is the first zig-zag.

The second zig-zag results from the fact that it is impossible to talk about Heidegger without using some of the key words he uses, and these key words are German and Greek (the relationship between German and Greek is a theme that runs through Heidegger's work from the beginning to end). The lecture has to zig-zag back and forth between using the words Heidegger himself uses and trying to explain those words accurately in English. Besides these extreme alternatives of using the German and the Greek words themselves and explaining those words in English, there are the alternatives of awkward translation and short paraphrase.

I hope that you will bear with these two zig-zaggings, the one between themes and their relationships and the other between German and Greek words and English words. The result of these compromises between trying to do justice to Heidegger's complexity and also trying to consider the occasion is no doubt, first, some simplification of Heidegger and, second, offering a little to everybody and not much to anybody.

I began by saying that this lecture is about some relationships among several themes in Heidegger. A theme can be related to another theme in various ways, among other ways by suppression of one theme by another, by reduction of one theme to another, by reversal of a theme, and by transposition of a theme into a new context. Heidegger weaves a complex web of suppressions and reductions, of reversals and transpositions.

The publication of course lectures given by Heidegger in Marburg in the 1920s, as well as an account, given by him in 1963 called "My Way to Phenomenology," confirms the importance of Aristotle and Husserl for the early Heidegger. A great deal of my lecture has to do with ambivalence and misinterpretation in Heidegger's relation to Aristotle and Husserl. Only toward the end does the lecture come to the comparison and contrast of Heidegger and Aquinas.

Both Heidegger and Aquinas distinguish "to be" from "being" and "beings." Likenesses and differences in the ways in which they take this distinction suggest another web, a web of comparison and contrast between Heidegger and Aquinas concerning the common theme of "to be," the most obscure of themes.

Suppression, reduction, reversal, transposition; ambivalence and misinterpretation; comparison and contrast—we will try to thread our way through this thicket in the hope of reaching a clearing.

INTRODUCTION

Heidegger has been persistently guilty of three misinterpretations. There may be others as well, but I wish to consider only the following three.

(1) The first misinterpretation is the reduction of Plato to the theme of *eidos* or form. Further themes in Plato, themes such as the *otherness* of kind to kind and the weaving together and carding apart of kinds, and, beyond that, the themes of both a unity beyond kinds, a unity which binds kinds together, and a "*not*" which is beyond the "not" of one kind not being another kind—to central themes in Plato such as these Heidegger seems blind.[1]

---

1. See Hans-Georg Gadamer, *Gesammelte Werke* (Tübingen: Mohr, 1985ff.) II, p. 12; III, pp. 16–22, 245–48, 302–3, 410–13; IV, p. 481; VI, pp. 129–53; VII, pp. 82, 280,

(2) The second misinterpretation is the reduction of creation as a theme in medieval thought to making or production and, closely related to that, the reduction of the difference between essence and existence to the issue of making "ideas" "real," to the producing of the "real" out of "ideas" or out of the possible. Idea as possibility-to-be-made-real is thus successor to *eidos* or form in the context of an apotheosis of making. Heidegger seems blind to the difference between being "out of possibility" and being "out of nothing," a difference central to the specificity of creation, which is not *ex possibili* but *ex nihilo*.

(3) The third misinterpretation is the reduction of the deepest theme in Husserl's thought to the theme of reflexivity or the objectification of subjectivity to itself. Heidegger seems blind to Husserl's deepest theme, the theme of the interplay of the presencing and absencing of presence and absence themselves as distinguished from that-which-is-present and that-which-is-absent.

Presence is not simply the same as that-which-is-present because that-which-is-present could be absent too and still be the same. That which can be either present or absent is the same, but presence and absence themselves are not the same, neither the same as each other nor taken together the same as that which is both present and absent. But presence and absence are not simply psychological either; they are too at one with that-which-*is*(-present) and that-which-*is*(-absent). To have been taken by this difference-in-unity between presence and that-which-is-present is to have presenced the presence itself of that-which-is-present.

We will return to this triple: presencing, presence, that-which-is-present. For the moment, however, note that presence is ambiguous. It is both presence of that-which-is-present and also itself, insofar as it itself is presenced, somehow a that-which-is-present.

Heidegger denies any indebtedness to Husserl's analysis of time.[2] Perhaps the reason for Heidegger's blindness to this theme in Husserl is that this theme is so crucial for Heidegger himself, but Heidegger transposes it into a very different way of speaking. Perhaps Heidegger occluded this theme in Husserl because Heidegger was searching for a more suitable way to speak about the theme, a way not still embed-

---

367. See Heidegger, *Gesamtausgabe* (Frankfurt am Main: Klostermann, 1975ff.), vol. 26, sec. 11 (b). See also Heidegger's praise of Plato's *Sophist*, vol. 34, pp. 68, 110, 305. See Scholium III, below.

2. "Über das Zeitverstandis in der Phänomenologie und im Denken der Seinsfrage," in *Phänomenologie—lebendig oder tot?*, ed. Helmut Gehrig (Karlsruhe: Badenia Verlag, 1969), p. 47; Gadamer, *Gesammelte Werke* III, p. 274.

ded, as it was for Husserl, despite Husserl's attempts at purification, in a matrix of terms redolent of psychology.

Husserl made a central issue of the difference between the psychological and the transcendental, and, further, he moved beyond the object-act-ego display of the transcendental. In connection with this difference and this move, he anticipated Heidegger's shift to the primacy of manifestation and hiddenness over the one to whom what-is-manifest and what-is-hidden is manifested and hidden. Husserl anticipated Heidegger's shift to the primacy of manifestation itself over the dative of manifestation, over the *mihi*, the "to me," the "to me" which seems to be a declination from the *ego*, the "I," but which Husserl himself reverses to the status of that out of which the ego comes about, the ego as the center of responsibility and as the recipient of objectifications. Manifestation has primacy over "to me," and "to me" has primacy over "I."

In retrospect, in looking back at Husserl from Heidegger, we can see that Husserl himself deconstructed the terminology of psychology, and to some extent also the terminology of the transcendental, from within, that is, by using it to say something strictly beyond its means.

Husserl's deepest theme, the theme of so-called "inner time-consciousness," is finally neither "inner" nor "temporal" nor "consciousness."[3] It is not "inner" because it is beyond the distinction between immanent and transcendent, for example, beyond the distinction between the act of seeing a white horse (the act is immanent) and the seen white horse itself (the object is transcendent). It is not "temporal," because it is beyond the object or the act which is present or absent and which therefore can be timed as "now" or "no longer" or "not yet." It is not "consciousness," because it is beyond the distinction between act and object, for example, beyond the distinction between an act of remembering and its object, which is the act of having seen a white horse, and also beyond the distinction between this act of having seen a white horse and its object, the seen white horse itself.

In Husserl's terminology, so-called "inner time-consciousness" is the unity articulated into primary showing (*Urimpression*) together with retention and protention,[4] and this unity is not an act-object unity,

---

3. See, for example, *Husserliana* vol. X, p. 333, l. 21–22; 371, 16; 382, 22.
4. Retention is *not* an *act* of remembering; protention is *not* an *act* of anticipating. On "inner time-consciousness" in Husserl, see the following: Robert Sokolowski, *Husserlian Meditations* (Evanston: Northwestern University Press, 1974), secs. 52–63, pp. 132–67; John Brough, "The Emergence of an Absolute Consciousness in Husserl's Early Writings on Time-Consciousness," *Man and World* 5 (1972), 298–326; Rudolf Bernet, "Is the Present Ever Present? Phenomenology and the Metaphysics of Presence,"

although act-object unity is the usual sense of intentionality. The primary showing is not an *act* which intends as its *objects acts* of retention and protention, and one articulated unit of the unity primary-showing-together-with-retention-and-protention intends other whole units in retention and in protention, but not as an *act* intends an *object* (Husserl calls this unusual intending *Längsintentionalität*). Primal presencing, primary showing, whatever *act* it may present or show (in *Querintentionalität*), is always also absencing into a presencing absénted or cleared out in retention and into a new primal presencing which itself has another presencing yet to come but still absent in protention. For Husserl this clearing out (in retention) and accepting (in protention) is more basic than any act-object achievement of the transcendental ego; it lets that ego living in such achievements come about.

This distention, Husserl's so-called "inner time-consciousness," the primary showing together with retention and protention, is in the last analysis the primal presencing/absencing of the presence/absence of that-which-is-present/absent. But to say this is to translate what Husserl said into a language we learn not from Husserl but from Heidegger. Husserl worked his analysis out using a psychology of the perception of tones and melodies; Heidegger, on the other hand, presents his analysis in *Being and Time* using themes like tools and death. The means of persuasion and demonstration are different. But what Husserl calls "the appearance of the flow to itself" is beyond the object-act-ego display, and so Heidegger's reduction of Husserl to the self-objectification of transcendental subjectivity is a misinterpretation.

On the other hand, we can see in retrospect why Heidegger braced

---

Research in Phenomenology 12 (1982), 85–112, and the German version, "Die ungegenwärtige Gegenwart. Anwesenheit und Abwesenheit in Husserls Analyse des Zeitbewußtseins," *Phänomenologische Forschungen* 14 (Freiburg/Munich: Karl Alber, 1983), pp. 16–57; "Die Frage nach dem Ursprung der Zeit bei Husserl und Heidegger," *Heidegger Studies* 3/4 (1987–88), 89–104, and the French version, "Origine du temps et temps originaire chez Husserl et Heidegger," *Revue philosophique de Louvain* 85 (1987), 499–521; Einleitung, Ergänzende Texte, *Husserliana*, Bd. X, Philosophische Bibliothek, Bd. 362 (Hamburg: Felix Meiner, 1985), pp. xlv–lvi, esp. lv–lvi. "La présence du passé dans l'analyse husserlienne de la conscience du temps," *Revue de Métaphysique et de Morale* 88 (1983), 178–98 (esp. 193), is another formulation of Bernet's criticism of Husserl for not doing what Bernet says he did do: Husserl (a) moved beyond intentionality as act-object correlation and therefore beyond reflection or self-objectification and (b) gave to difference and absence a co-primacy with sameness and presence. See also "Differenz und Anwesenheit . . . ," *Phänomenologische Forschungen* 18 (Freiburg/Munich: Karl Alber, 1986), pp. 51–112, esp. 80–81, 94. An exposition of admirable precision: John Brough, "Husserl's Phenomenology of Time-Consciousness," in *Husserl's Phenomenology: A Textbook*, ed. J. N. Mohanty and Wm. R. McKenna (Washington, D.C.: University Press of America, 1989), pp. 249–89. Brough's review of Bernet's introduction to the Meiner edition: *Husserl Studies* 4 (1987), 243–66.

himself against the terminology Husserl still used. Gadamer recalls[5] that Heidegger made his Aristotle strong in his very opposition to Aristotle; but perhaps Heidegger was so close to Husserl, in contrast to his distance from Aristotle, that he made Husserl weak in order to free himself from the matrix in which Husserl was still to some extent entangled, the matrix of the language of acts and their objects, especially the objects which acts themselves become when they are reflected on or objectified by other acts.

These, then, are misinterpretations of which Heidegger is persistently guilty: (1) he reduces Plato to the theme of *eidos* or form; (2) he reduces creation to an apotheosis of making as realization out of possibility; and (3) he reduces Husserl's last word to the self-objectification of transcendental subjectivity.

In addition to considering these three misinterpretations, I wish to add consideration of an issue of ambiguity and an issue of comparison and contrast:

(4) The ambiguity is in Heidegger's use of a crucial term, *Lichtung*, a term which is ambiguous because Heidegger uses it to mean both clearing up or bringing to light or making clear, on the one hand, and, on the other hand, he also and finally uses it to mean clearing away or lightening or opening up: *etwas lichten, etwas frei und offen machen*.[6]

(5) The comparison and contrast are between *Sein* for Heidegger and *esse* for Aquinas. Both terms are accurately and awkwardly translated "to be" as distinguished from "being" and "beings." (*Sein* is to *Seiendes* as *esse* is to *ens*.) Comparison is suggested because both Heidegger and Aquinas make strong claims for "to be" as distinguished from "being" and "beings." But contrast is suggested because Aquinas sets *esse* against the foil of essence, essence as the principle that receives *esse* and in receiving *esse* limits it, *esse* of itself "being," so to speak, unlimited. Heidegger, on the other hand, sets *Sein* as the interplay of presence/absence themselves (or itself) against the foil of that-which-is(-present/absent). Recall the triple: presencing of the presence of

---

5. Gadamer, *Gesammelte Werke* II, pp. 485–86; III, p. 199; *Philosophische Lehrjahre* (Frankfurt am Main: Klostermann, 1977), p. 36.

6. *Zur Sache des Denkens* (Tübingen: Max Niemeyer, 1969), p. 72.; Martin Heidegger—Eugen Fink, *Heraklit* (Frankfurt am Main: Klostermann, 1970), p. 260; *Zur Frage nach der Bestimmung der Sache des Denkens* (St. Gallen: Erker, 1984), p. 17. In these three late texts (made public between 1964 and 1966) Heidegger is emphatic about the difference between *Lichtung* and light in the sense of bright-dark. *Lichtung* is *Gewährnis des Freien für Anwesen und Verweilen von Anwesendem* and *das Offene für alles An- und Abwesende*: the granting of the space free and open for the interplay of presencing/absencing and the presenced/the absenced. Cf. *Sein und Zeit*, 14. Auflage, p. 133 (a,b,c: p. 442), pp. 350–51. See note 13 below.

that-which-is(-present), a triple which distinguishes from one another pre*sencing* of the pre*sence* of the pre*sent*. And note that "pre*sencing*" is a participle with both verbal and nominal senses (cf. "Forgetting your umbrella is a nuisance."), "pre*sence*" is a noun, and "pre*sent*" is both an adjective and a noun. So we come to *grammatica speculativa,* the mirroring of the highest themes in grammatical forms.

EXPLANATORY NOTE ON *SEIN-DASEIN-SEIENDES* AND *ALĒTHEIA*

A.

In English we use the infinitive as a noun ("To err is human, to forgive divine."), but we do not use the definite article with the infinitive used as a noun; we do not say "*the* to-err" or "*the* to-be"; we have no articular infinitive. German, however, can use the neuter definite article (*das*) with the infinitive, which is then capitalized because it is used as a noun (all German nouns are capitalized). The German infinitive *sein* means "to be." Using it as a noun, capitalized, and with the neuter definite article, gives the form *das Sein:* "the to-be."

The present participle of *sein,* which is the infinitive of the verb "to be," is in its verbal or adjectival form *seiend* and in its neuter singular nominal form *Seiendes* or, with the neuter definite article, *das Seiende.* As the nominal form, it is capitalized. For Heidegger it means "being(s) as distinguished from 'the to-be' or from *das Sein.*" The translation of the title of Heidegger's book *Sein und Zeit* as *Being and Time* blurs this distinction.

Da is an adverb meaning the one root-meaning common to both "here" and "there." Using it as a prefix with the infinitive *sein* and taking the compound as a noun, and so capitalizing it, gives the form *Dasein,* which means something like "the availability (in withdrawnness) of 'to-be' as such." *Dasein* is the central term of Heidegger's book *To Be and Time,* and it is wisely left untranslated.

The perfect passive participle of the infinitive *sein* is *gewesen,* a form related to an infinitive form of the verb "to be" which is no longer used: *wesan* or *wesen.* However, this old form of the infinitive "to be" still occurs in compounds: *anwesen, abwesen:* "to be present (to . . .)" and "to be absent (from . . .)" or "to be presenced (to . . .)" and "to be absenced (from . . .)."

The *-sens* root of the Latin forms *praesens, absens* derives from *sant,* the present participle of *as,* the Sanskrit verb "to be." *Prae* means "in front (of)"; the idiom *prae se ferre* means "to show, exhibit, discover, manifest." *Ab* means "away (from)."

Dasein can thus be translated as something like "the availability (in withdrawnness) of the interplay of presence to . . . /absence from . . ." or "the availability (in withdrawnness) of the interplay of (to be) available to . . . /(to be) withdrawn from . . .".

In summary form:

sein:	to be
da:	here/there
Dasein:	to be (available) here/to be (withdrawn) there
wesen:	to be
an/ab:	to/from
anwesen/abwesen:	to be (present) to/to be (absent) from
sens:	being
prae/ab:	in front of/away from
praesens/absens:	being in front of/being away from

Presence/absence taken as such or *das Sein* is to be distinguished from that-which-is(-present/absent) or from *das Seiende*. Heidegger calls this difference "the ontological difference." This difference is formulated in section 2 of *To Be and Time:* "The to-be of being(s) 'is' not itself a being."[7]

For Heidegger the ". . ." of the "to . . ./from . . ." of "presence to . . ./absence from . . ." is a reversal away from subjectivity without being thereby a reversal toward objectivity. *Das Sein* appropriates (as) *Dasein* or avails itself (*braucht:* "needs"/"uses") of or through *Dasein*. *Das Sein* needs or uses a being among beings, the being to whom and from whom beings-which-are are manifest and hidden. Presence/absence brings about the *who*, so to speak, for its *to* whom/*from* whom. Only because *das Sein* "is" the interplay of presence/absence can there "be" human beings who can represent things to themselves and manipulate things for themselves in the derivative and reduced senses of *logos* and *technē*.

B.

Alētheia is a Greek compound with three elements.

As the center part of the compound, *lēthē* means something like "forgotten, covered (over), concealed, veiled, inevident, hidden, obscure."

With a prefix *a-* for "un-" or "not" and a suffix *-ia* for "-ness" or "-th" or "-ty," *lēthē* is the root of the word *alētheia*, "truth" or "verity" understood as "*un*covered*ness*, *un*concealed*ness*, *un*hidden*ness*." If *lēthē*

---

7. See p. 195 and pp. 248–52 of Volume 26 of the Complete Edition.

is thought of as the *un*articulated and the *in*evident, then, through a double reversal, *alētheia*, as the *not-un*-articulated and the *not-in*-evident, would be the root of the articulation and the evidencing in *logos:* truth and "logic" somehow go together.

EPIGRAPH

"*Logos und technē aber sind, ganz weit genommen, diejenigen Verhaltungen, in denen sich das Seiende überhaupt zunächst offenbart, so zwar daß in diesem Horizont die Idee des Seins zunächst sich ausbildet.*" "But *logos* and *technē*, taken in the widest sense, are those involvements in which being(s) as such first come(s) to light, so that it is within this horizon that the idea of to-be itself is first formed." Complete Edition, volume 26 (Course Lectures given in the Summer Semester of 1928, Marburg), p. 146.

TWO SUMMARIES

A. Logos

Summary of Course Lectures given in the Winter Semester of 1925/6, Marburg; sections 11 through 14 in the context of section 10, volume 21, Complete Edition.

According to Heidegger's 1925/6 lectures, the primary synthesis is the unthematic synthesis of something together with whatever we take it *as* (being) useful *for*. Concern is the context of this primary synthesis, the synthesis called the interpretative *as*. This primary unthematic synthesis can, through a shift to a secondary concern, be suppressed and replaced by the thematic predicative synthesis: saying something *as* (being) a characteristic *of* something: S is articulated as *being* P; P is said to be *true* of S. When this synthesis of predication is itself evidenced or verified, then there is a third synthesis, a synthesis of merely *saying* P to be true of S ("empty intention") together with indeed *seeing* P to be true of S ("filling intention"). When in turn and finally this synthesis, the synthesis of evidence or verification, is itself thematized and evidenced, then we focus on the *is* or *to be* itself as *being-truth* or on *being as truthing* (cf. Husserl, *Logical Investigations* VI, secs. 36–39).

B. Technē

Summary of Course Lectures given in the Summer Semester of 1927, Marburg; sections 10 through 12 in the context of section 9(b)(c), volume 24, Complete Edition.

According to Heidegger's 1927 lectures, the genealogy of existence as different from essence is the achievedness of the finished product insofar as the product is brought to a stand over against the producer and over against the producer's "mere idea" of the product to be produced: *existentia* is understood as *extra causam stare*. As so achieved, the product is there in the context of primary concern, there to be used, and it is brought about out of material that has not been produced, out of nature as the limit of production. What is placed or set up as standing there over against for use can then, through a shift to a secondary concern, the theoretical concern, be taken as being something there for contemplation to gaze on as *being true*.

PART I

Heidegger uses Husserl (especially *Logical Investigations* VI, secs. 36–39) for an exposition of Aristotle's analysis of *logos* (especially in *Metaphysics* Book IX, Chapter 10): declaration is both characterization (or predicational synthesis) and verification (or evidential synthesis). Heidegger then criticizes Aristotle's analysis of *logos* for having suppressed the roots of declaration in use, use flowing from concern. Gazing is secondary to using. Heidegger shows the roots of *logos* in *technē*, that is, in *technē* as producing products to be used. The predicative truth of something characterized as being *so* is secondary to and rooted in the prepredicative good of something taken as being useful *for*.

Heidegger also criticizes an understanding of the articulation of being into a difference between essence and existence in the context of creation *ex nihilo* by reducing that articulation back to roots in Aristotle's analysis of *technē*, that is, in *technē* as producing products by bringing them to a stand over against the producer. Heidegger suppresses the importance of creation *ex nihilo* by assimilating it to producing understood as bringing to be the real out of the possible, producing understood as translation of an essence from the status of possibility to the status or stand of reality. Heidegger suppresses creation *ex nihilo*, as contrasted with making *ex possibili*, as a context for understanding the articulation of being into essence and existence. Creation is reduced to *making* "ideas" or possible beings into "real" beings, to *making* "real" beings out of the material of possible beings or out of "mere ideas."

Heidegger also suppresses the context of Aristotle's analysis of *technē*, that is, Heidegger suppresses nature and contemplation. More precisely, he suppresses nature as *more* than just the limit of production, that out of which products are produced. He suppresses nature as being for contemplation, and he suppresses nature as suspended (1072b13–14) from that contemplation which is *best* because it is unity without articulation and presence without absence: *noēsis* beyond *logos*. (Heidegger analyzes *Metaphysics* Theta 10 in section 9 of volume 31 of the Complete Edition.)

In *To Be and Time* Heidegger introduces a non-Aristotelian context for his analysis of *technē:* death as the limit of presencing out of absence. Each one's death cannot be presenced for each one out of its absence, but each one is always already in anticipation his necessarily still absent death. Death is the limit of *Dasein, Dasein* which is concern (*Sorge*), oscillating between presence and absence.[8] Concern, in turn, is the context of use, use which is the context of produced products, which are brought to a stand over against the producer.

These three criticisms, namely,

(1) the criticism of *logos* because *logos* obscures our primary access to the world through use flowing from concern;

(2) the criticism of creation as an apotheosis of making;

(3) the criticism of *noēsis* as unity without articulation and presence without absence;

and these three suppressions, namely,

(4) the suppression of the roots of *logos* in *technē*, a suppression which Heidegger criticizes [(4) corresponds to (1)];

(5) Heidegger's own suppression of creation *ex nihilo*, in favor of making *ex possibili*, as a context for understanding the articulation of being into essence and existence, a suppression of creation *ex nihilo* by reducing it to roots in *technē*, to an apotheosis of making [(5) corresponds to (2)];

(6) Heidegger's own suppression of nature *for* contemplation and of nature in the highest sense *as* contemplation as contexts for *logos* and *technē* [(6) corresponds to (3)];

—all these criticisms and suppressions are placed by Heidegger in the service of an understanding of *Sein* and *alētheia*, an understanding which parallels both Husserl's treatment of empty intentions and of retention (paralleled by *lēthē* in Heidegger) and Husserl's treatment of transcendental subjectivity at its core, "the appearance of the flow

---

8. This oscillation is the *formal* ontological structure of *phronēsis*, spanning *hexis* and the possible, with the agent as *archē* "between" them; see Aristotle, *Nicomachean Ethics* 1140b27–30. Gadamer confirms the importance of Heidegger's analysis of *phronēsis* in the 1920s. See note 5 above.

to itself" or so-called "inner time-consciousness" (paralleled by *Sein* in Heidegger). Heidegger's understanding of *Sein* and *alētheia* can be formulated as the presencing/absencing (taken as such) *of* the presence/absence (taken as such) *of* the present/absent, that is, of that-which-is(-present/absent). What is the sense of this triple: the presencing *of* the presence *of* the present?

The white horse is not yet here; the white horse is still absent.

The white horse appears on the scene; the white horse, which was at first absent, although expected, is now present.

The presence of the white horse is to be distinguished from the white horse itself, which is present, because the same white horse which is present was absent too, and its presence is not its absence. So the absence too of the white horse is to be distinguished from the white horse itself, which is now present after first having been absent.

The same white horse can be both present and absent, and presence and absence are not each other. Neither the presence alone of the white horse nor the absence alone of the white horse can be the same as the white horse itself. And both together, united in their difference, are not the white horse either; the white horse is not the same as its presence/absence. But neither is the white horse without its presence/absence, just as they are not without it. What would presence or absence be without the presence of . . . and the absence of . . . ? And what would a being be without presence/absence? The presence/absence of the white horse, to be the being the white horse, is not on the same line as the white of the white horse or as the horse of the white horse. Yet the white and the horse are that-which-*is* (-present/absent). And if to be the being the white horse absorbed or exhausted "to be," then there could not be the being a red rose as well as the being a white horse. But can we ever take "to be" *only* as "to be" and *not* as "the to-be" *of* being(s),[9] *of* white horses and red roses?

We in our analysis have just been presencing for ourselves the presence itself and taken as such of the white horse, which is present. Soon this presencing of the presence of the white horse will itself be absenced, forgotten, even though the white horse itself may still be present. We will forget to discriminate the white horse present from its presence itself, a presence which we in our analysis have just been presencing because we were taken by the difference between presence and that which is present.

9. For a time Heidegger used an old spelling, *Seyn*, for "to be" only as "to be." Heidegger's *Seyn* and Aquinas's *esse commune* are *in this sense* similar: both mean "to be" only as "to be" and as distinguished but not separated from "the to-be" *of* being(s).

We in our analysis have been engaged in an act or an achieving, a philosophical act, which can be initiated and stopped and which can be forgotten and remembered (and controverted). But the primal presencing with absencing, the primal showing together with retention and protention, cannot be gained or lost by us, cannot be begun or ended by us. Inexorably and gratuitously it presences and absences the whole network of presencing and absencing *acts* or achievings and their presenced and absenced *objects* or themes, and out of it comes about what we call "I" as the center of responsibility which initiates and as the recipient of objectifications which are displayed. We cannot represent or manipulate the bringing about of us, we who can represent or manipulate beings only because we are caught up in the web woven by the interplay of primal presencing/absencing happily beyond our control.

In 1909/11 (according to Bernet's dating of crucial manuscripts, revising Boehm's dating) Husserl, in thinking about what he called "inner time-consciousness," clarified a distinction between acts or achievements of presencing (for example, acts of seeing the white horse and acts of remembering having seen the white horse), on the one hand, and, on the other hand, a flowing-away-and-gathering-together which is the presencing/absencing *of* those very acts or achievements of presencing, but *not* in the same space as they. Husserl saw that this flowing-and-gathering is *not* in the same space as acts or achievements of seeing and of remembering having seen the white horse. This space of acts of seeing the white horse and of remembering having seen the white horse is the space where reflexivity takes place, the space where I can think myself having thought. Even *my act* (as an owned achieving), my *philosophical* act of presencing the presence itself of the white horse is within this space open to reflexivity. But the flowing-and-gathering itself, the primal interplay of the presencings and absencing *of* all presencing *acts* (precisely as having this genitive "*of* . . . *acts*," it is called by Husserl *Querintentionalität*), even *of* my philosophical *act* of presencing presence itself, this flowing-and-gathering itself is a space different from and beyond the whole space where reflexivity takes place. It is beyond the *cogitatum-cogitatio-ego cogitans* and the *ego cogito me cogitantem cogitatum*, that is, beyond the subject-object distinction and beyond the objectification of subjectivity to itself. For Husserl the flowing-and-gathering, primal distention and interplay, primal presencing absencing as retention and protention, and thus presencing itself presenced as absented in retention and absent in protention, all this is beyond and different from presenced and presencing *acts*, whether perceptual, memorial, or philosophical.[10]

It is true that Husserl spoke of this space of flowing-and-gathering using terms of the language of psychology and of transcendental subjectivity as the unifying pole of acts achieving the presentation of objects as well as of acts achieving objectifying presentation of those acts which achieve the presentation of objects. But then Heidegger too had to struggle to free a language of "to be" itself and taken as such from the language used to speak about being and beings. Both Husserl and Heidegger struggled to free the *significatum* from the inappropriate *modus significandi*. Heidegger freed himself from the language of what he calls "metaphysics," which according to Heidegger understands "to be" only as "*of* being(s)" and not by itself and taken as such, but he freed himself from this language by recapitulating it. Perhaps Husserl freed himself less from the language of reflexivity, the language of the objectification of subjectivity to itself. But Heidegger paid a heavy price for his greater freedom from an inappropriate language: Heidegger's twists or tropes of his base language sometimes carry him to the very edge of that communication without which there is no language at all.

PART II

Heidegger later transposes the analysis of *logos* into the context of *Sein* and *alētheia* in his interpretation of *logos* in Heraclitus[11] as the collectedness in which presence/absence comes about, and he later transposes the analysis of *technē* into the context of *Sein* and *alētheia* in his interpretation of technology (*Technik*) in terms of *Ge-stell:* the produced is brought forth and set up, set up in being clear or in standing forth as being manifest. The apotheosis of *making* products leads by way of *making clear* to an obscuring of nature by representation and manipulation.

In these interpretations of Heraclitus and of technology, Heraclitus early and technology late, linked by the theme of making clear or

---

10. The distinction between the philosophical act of presencing the presence of that-which-is(-present) and the primal interplay of presencing/absencing corresponds roughly to the distinction Heidegger makes between *Seinsverständnis* and *Seinsgeschehnis* in "Zur Kritik der Vorlesung," *Einführung in die Metaphysik*, volume 40 of the Complete Edition, p. 219.

11. See sec. 8 of the course lectures of the Summer Semester of 1943 and sec. 8 of the course lectures of the Summer Semester of 1944, both in volume 55 of the Complete Edition. These last Freiburg lectures rejoin the early Marburg lectures by way of a reversal and recovery in a new context.

bringing to manifestness, Heidegger reverses his early suppression of nature and contemplation as the context of *logos* and *technē* by recovering *logos* and *technē* in the context of nature and contemplation, themselves now recovered in the light of *Sein* and *alētheia*.

Heidegger now understands nature as the interplay of presence/absence or of manifestation/hiddenness, and he understands contemplation as taking or accepting both the coming about of the difference (*Austrag*) in the interplay itself and the difference between the interplay and that which it needs/uses: that-which-*is* as now standing out as made clear to. . . .

Heidegger speaks of an obscuring of *Sein* (*Seinsvergessenheit*), an absencing of the interplay of presence/absence itself in favor of that-which-is(-present/absent). The presencing of presence/absence itself almost necessarily turns presence/absence itself into a that-which-is(-*now*-)(-present). The reversal of this necessity of turning presence into something present in the present, the reversal of this necessity of favoring that-which-is(-*now*-)(-present) over presence/absence itself, this reversal Heidegger calls "the other beginning."

The other beginning is a recapitulation of the first beginning, the beginning with Anaximander, Parmenides, and Heraclitus. This other beginning is the recapitulation which comes at the end of what was begun by the first beginning. The first beginning lived in *physis* and *logos* and *alētheia* as the interplay of presence/absence or manifestness/hiddenness, and it also lived in the pull toward turning presence/absence or manifestness/hiddenness into a that-which-is(-present/absent) or that-which-is(-manifest/hidden). The first beginning lived in the pull toward favoring making clear that-which-is. The first beginning ended with technology. The other beginning recapitulates that first beginning with a reversal favoring the presencing of the interplay of presence/absence or manifestness/hiddenness itself as distinguished from its fall into that-which-is(-present or -manifest).

The first beginning lived in the manifestness of that-which-is(-manifest), but that manifestness itself and as such remained withdrawn in obscurity. The other beginning overcomes that withdrawnness into obscurity and brings the manifestness itself of that-which-is(-manifest) to clarity or manifestation out of obscurity. *And it tries to do this without falling under the sway of the necessity to turn this manifested manifestness itself into another something among others which has now been made clear to.* . . .

PART III

Heidegger later moves beyond his theme of *Sein* and *alētheia* toward what he calls *Lichtung*, which finally means not so much a clearing up out of obscurity or a clarification or a lighting up as rather a clearing away or a lightening up, leaving room or space beyond the interplay of presencing/absencing. The theme of *Lichtung* goes beyond both Aristotle and Husserl. It goes beyond Heidegger's recapitulation and deconstruction of Aristotle's *logos* and *technē* and beyond Husserl's so-called "inner time-consciousness." But it does not go as far as an understanding of the articulation of being into essence and existence in the context of creation, the gift of *esse ex nihilo*.

Although *Lichtung* is beyond the interplay of presencing/absencing, it is almost impossible to speak of it except in terms of absencing (*Abwesen*), withdrawal (*Entzug*), reserve (*Vorenthalt*), hiddenness (*lēthē*). Like Husserl before him, Heidegger has to use inappropriate language to speak about something that is strange (*atopon*) because it is so simple. He has to borrow language appropriate to what is more familiar because it is less simple. This expropriated and troped language strains to bring to speech what is beyond its resources.

Before the move beyond the interplay of presencing/absencing into *Lichtung* as clearing away, there is a shift of accent within that interplay itself: truthing or clearing up out of obscurity or presencing out of absence is not just a working *against* absence or withdrawal or obscurity. Rather it is just as much *letting* obscurity and withdrawal and absence *be* as that out of which clarity and availability and presence come forth: hiding (*Verbergung*) is protecting (*Bergung*), protecting from the excessive demand for making clear, the demand for exhaustive clarity, a demand that pushes toward manipulation of the represented.

CONCLUSION

The *subsistens* of Aquinas's creator God, *esse subsistens*, means, in contrast to *esse commune*, in contrast to *esse completum* ("full") *et simplex sed non subsistens* (*De potentia Dei* I, 1), self-sufficiency, non-receivability in an other. *Esse commune*, in contrast to *esse subsistens*, is *componendum alteri:* it is to be received in an other, in an essence as other to *esse*. Although *esse* as *esse commune* is considered or taken without that other with which it is to be composed, nevertheless it has a unity not reducible to the unity owed merely to considering it without that other with which it is composed. For Aquinas the foil to *esse* is the limiting essence with which the *esse* is composed, such that the compound, the *ens* as the unity of *esse* and essence, has subsistence or self-sufficiency, which neither *esse* nor essence can enjoy alone. For Heidegger, on the other hand, the foil to *Sein* as the interplay of presence/absence itself is that-which-is(-present/absent): the to-be is the to-be *of* being(s).

And although Heidegger's *Sein* as the interplay of presence/absence is prior to its "to . . ./from . . . ," it is nevertheless bound back into the "to . . ./from. . . ." In this way too Heidegger's *Sein*, like Aquinas's *esse*, is *componendum alteri*, to be together with an other. Just as Aquinas's *esse*, if it is not *subsistens*, needs or uses essence if there is to be *ens subsistens*, that is, if *esse* is to be "the to-be" *of* being(s), so Heidegger's interplay of presence/absence needs or uses (*braucht*) its dative of manifestation/hiddenness. It needs or uses its "manifest *to* . . ./hidden *from* . . ."; it needs or uses a being among beings, the being to whom and from whom beings-which-are are manifest and hidden. And although Heidegger exhorts us to think "the to-be," *das Sein*, by taking it as itself and not only as "the to-be" *of* being(s), and although this genitive, "*of* being(s)," can be suppressed or occluded, so to speak, in order to focus on "the to-be" itself and taken as such, yet the "*of* being(s)" cannot be done away with, any more than for Aquinas the essence *in* which created *esse* is received (in order that there be beings) or *with* which it is composed and *by* which it is limited can be done away with or reduced to nothing at all.

Heidegger takes presence/absence as "the to-be" itself and as such of beings, "the to-be" to which we, as datives of manifestation and as coming to represent and to manipulate beings, are subsidiary, although never superfluous. Heidegger in the end goes beyond *Sein* as the interplay of presence/absence. And he goes beyond the presencing/absencing itself of this presence/absence of that-which-is(-present/absent). But of this beyond, this *Lichtung*, this clearing away beyond all presencing/absencing, he can only say that it is the context for the interplay of presencing/absencing, a context both cleared of that interplay and yet readable only as translated into the text of that interplay, a translation which always reduces and thus traduces. This context beyond the interplay, this context of which we almost have to be silent or of which we can speak only inappropriately or in bad translation, is the proper sense of *Lichtung*, a sense reached only through and beyond, first, distinguishing presencing/absencing from the presence/absence which is presenced/absenced (and thus reduced to a that-which-is(-present/absent)), and, second, understanding absencing as more a protection (*Bergung, Wahrnis*) of presencing, a protection protecting presencing from the tendency to separate itself

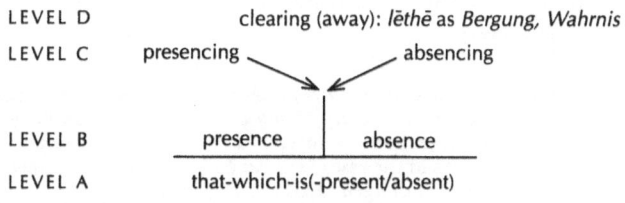

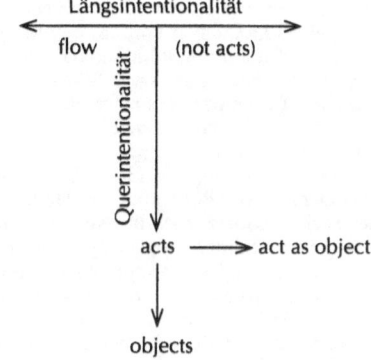

off from the absencing over which its solitary splendor would then triumph. Absencing is more a protection of presencing than an obstacle which presencing fights against in order to overcome it by translating it into nothing but presence.

Lichtung beyond all interplay of presencing/absencing, even beyond the interplay in which absencing protects presencing, this proper sense of *Lichtung* cannot itself "be," and above all it cannot "be" as closed to *esse subsistens,* but thereof Heidegger is silent.

It seems that we have come to the end without having spoken about a central theme in the later Heidegger: *Ereignis*.[12] However, "itself, taken as such and distinguished from . . . ; proper, appropriate" are words that have been often used, and they are the meaning of the

12. See the account of the 1962 seminar on the 1962 lecture "Time and To Be" (*Zur Sache des Denkens,* pp. 27–60).

word *eigen*,[13] a word that Heidegger hears in *Ereignis*. So in the end saying "clearing away the inappropriate" (*Lichtung*) says "letting come into its own" (*Ereignis*).

13. *Eigen* as in *eigens, eignen, eigentlich, eigentümlich*. *Ereignis* has the same root as *Auge*, "eye." Just as *Lichtung* has the ambiguity *Licht/leicht* (*leukós/elakús*), so *Ereignis* has for Heidegger the ambiguity *Auge/eigen*. As "bright" is to "eye," so "cleared away" is to "appropriate." Heidegger says in the essay "Die Kehre": "*Ereignis ist eignende Eräugnis.*" See *Die Technik und die Kehre* (Pfullingen: Neske, 1962), p. 44.
The "four further seminars" referred to in the first paragraph of the Preface are published as *Vier Seminare* (Frankfurt am Main: Klostermann, 1977).
Sec. 7(a) of the appendix to Volume 45 (Freiburg Course Lectures of the Winter Semester 1937/8), pp. 209–11, moves within the whole complex of (1) the interplay of (a) presencing/absencing of (b) the presenced/the absenced; (2) withdrawal (*Entzug*) as protection (*Bergung*); and (3) *Lichtung* as both (a) bound into brightness (*Helle*) and (b) openness for the interplay of manifesting/hiding and the manifest/the hidden.
In 1937/8 (Vol. 45, p. 209) Heidegger says: "Wir sprechen von einer Waldlichtung, einer freien, hellen Stelle." In the passages referred to above in note 6, passages made public almost thirty years later, he says: "Das Lichte im Sinne des Freien und Offenen hat weder sprachlich noch in der Sache etwas mit dem Adjektivum 'licht' gemeinsam, das 'hell' bedeutet." "Haben Lichtung und Licht überhaupt etwas miteinander zu tun? Offenbar nicht." "Das Lichte in der Bedeutung des Hellen und das Lichte der Lichtung sind nicht nur in der Sache, sondern auch im Wort verschieden."
See also in the Complete Edition: Vol. 29/30, sec. 67, pp. 405–6, and sec. 76, pp. 530–31; Vol. 33, sec. 14(b) and sec. 20, pp. 201–3, 206.
Aquinas distinguishes *esse divinum, cui additio non fit et non fieri potest* from *esse commune, cui additio non fit sed fieri potest*. Not only is the *additio* (= *coarctatio*: limitation by essence) possible, it is necessary if there be beings. See *Summa theologiae* I 3, 4, ad 1, and *De potentia Dei* VII 2, ad 6.

13
The Death of Charm and the Advent of Grace: Waugh's *Brideshead Revisited*

> Fiction is the concrete expression of mystery—mystery that is lived. Catholics believe that all creation is good and that evil is the wrong use of good and that without Grace we use it wrong most of the time. It's almost impossible to write about supernatural Grace in fiction. We almost have to approach it negatively.[1]

Brideshead Revisited has been criticized for being lush, ornamental, and sentimental in style, on the one hand, and, on the other hand, for theological harshness. It could be said that the book oscillates between a surface romanticism and an intrusive eschatology or even that it falls apart into these two extremes. Has the earlier Waugh, taut and funny, given way to a combination of gluttony and bigotry?

My concern is to make the case that this criticism is a distortion. It misses the heart of Waugh's achievement: to have made a work in which the integrities of both art and faith are respected in their interaction. Indeed, they are respected precisely because of their interaction. The richness of the style and the stringency of the theology interact and thus intensify each other.

The book[2] has been made into a film. The colors and the intona-

---

1. Flannery O'Connor, in a letter of 10 March 1956. "A novel dealing with conversion is the most difficult the fiction writer can assign himself." *The Presence of Grace* (Athens: The University of Georgia Press, 1983), p. 16.
2. The British edition was published in 1945 by Chapman and Hall; the revised British edition was published in 1960. The American edition was published in 1945 by Little, Brown and Company. The film was made by Granada Television of England and first shown in this country by the Public Broadcasting Service in the spring of 1982. On the memorandum Waugh wrote while in Hollywood between October 1946 and February 1947 during negotiations with M-G-M about filming the book, see Pacificus Kennedy, "Romance and Redemption in 'Brideshead Revisited,'" *America* (1 May 1982), 334–36. The complete text of the memorandum, dated 18 February 1947, is printed in Jeffrey Heath, "*Brideshead:* The Critics and the Memorandum," *English Studies* 56

tions, the scenes and the acting of the film enrich the words of the book, just as a portrait helps us to see the one portrayed more clearly, but it is the text which is Waugh's work, and it remains the proper object of analysis.

Although the book has been well served by the fidelity of the film, I have one criticism: the newness and the bad taste of the chapel (38–39, 92, 351) are lost in the film, in which Sebastian says to Charles, "Papa had it *restored* for Mama as a wedding present." This may seem a small thing, but we shall see later why it is not.

I begin my analysis with a distinction which is basic, simple, obvious, old-fashioned, and in some quarters quite out of fashion: the distinction between what is presented and how it is presented. This distinction can be made variously: as the distinction between what is seen and both the angles of vision and the selection and sequence of views (when we see the hand moved closer to and farther from the eye, we do not see it as swelling and shrinking); as the distinction between what is represented and the ways and means of representing; as the distinction between the narrative which tells about a course of events and the course of events itself. The narrative is both drawn from—it has its source in the course of events which it narrates—and is withdrawn from—it is distanced from the course of events which it narrates.

Graham Greene formulates the distinction between art and life: "One cannot separate literature and life.... The form, the arrangement, ... separates art from mere realistic reporting however vivid. Fielding lifted life out of its setting and arranged it for the delight of all who loved symmetry."[3] And Waugh himself:

So in my future books there will be two things to make them unpopular: a preoccupation with style and the attempt to represent man more fully, which, to me, means only one thing, man in his relation to God.... I believe that you can only leave God out by making your characters pure abstractions. Countless admirable writers, perhaps some of the best in the world, succeed in this.... They try to represent the whole human mind and soul and yet omit its determining character—that of being God's creature.[4]

As for Greene "art" is to "life," so for Waugh "style" is to "God." In other words, the artfully represented course of events includes the gift

---

(1975), 222–30. On drafts and revisions, see Robert Murray Davis, *Evelyn Waugh, Writer* (Oklahoma: Pilgrim Press, 1981), pp. 107–85. Page references in parentheses are to the American edition.

3. Graham Greene, "Fielding and Sterne," *Collected Essays* (London: Penguin Books, 1981), pp. 67, 74.

4. Evelyn Waugh, "Fan-Fare," *A Little Order*, ed. Donat Gallagher (Boston: Little, Brown and Company, American edition, 1980), pp. 31–32. See p. 124.

and the call, the partnership and the exchange between God and man, man and God.

How has Waugh dealt with this difficult and delicate task, a task "ambitious, perhaps intolerably presumptuous,"[5] the task of representing in a work of art the workings of grace?

Having recalled the distinction and relation between art and life, and noting that for Waugh the life to be represented by his art includes "the workings of the divine purpose,"[6] and "the operation of divine grace,"[7] I now formulate my thesis: first, the themes presented or represented in *Brideshead Revisited* are memory and reversal; second, the structural devices, the representing means for the presentation of those themes, are framing, which presents memory, and mirroring, which presents reversal; and third, there is a fittingness, a congruence, an aptness between the presented themes and the presenting structural devices, an aptness which is the source of the proper, the distinguishing, the discriminating pleasure we take in the work.

The very title of the work brings together the two themes, memory and reversal: Brideshead revisited, memories awakened by unexpectedly seeing again a great house, seeing it again after having left it behind, seeing a great house fallen on dark times, remembering a once-beautiful house now seen marred and put to unexpected uses. What is remembered was full, but what is seen, and the situation of seeing it, are empty. Memory itself is a kind of reversal, "between two realities and two dreams" (15). From the point of view of the reality of remembered past sweetness, present desolation seems merely a dream; but reversed, seen from the point of view of the reality of present desolation, remembered past sweetness seems merely a dream. There is a shift back and forth between the remembering present and the remembered past. "Which was the mirage, which the palpable earth?" (16; cf. 169).

The work is the presentation, through the devices of framing and mirroring, of Charles remembering the story of the reversals, the conversions, of others leading to his own reversal and conversion. Reversal is a turn toward the opposite, an unexpected turning into the opposite, a shift, for instance, from looking forward to looking backward and then again to looking forward, or a shift from joy to sadness and then back again from sadness to joy.

The theme of memory is presented in the contrast between narrating time—thirty hours, the time of the framing Prologue-Epilogue—

---

5. Evelyn Waugh, "Warning," dustjacket of the 1945 British edition.
6. Ibid.
7. Evelyn Waugh, "Preface," 1960 British edition.

and narrated time—sixteen years, the time of the framed Books I and II. The Prologue-Epilogue covers thirty hours in the early spring of 1943, and Books I and II cover sixteen years from the spring of 1923 to the summer of 1939.

The work is divided into two Books;[8] the titles of the two Books tell of reversal, and the first words of each of the Books tell of memory. Book I is entitled "Et in Arcadia Ego": I, death, hold sway even in the midst of delight (42); Book II is entitled "A Twitch upon the Thread":[9] running away and being called back (220). Book I begins "'I have been here before,' I said; I had been there before" (21); Book II begins "My theme is memory, that winged host that soared about me one grey morning of war-time" (225).

Let us return to the theme of reversal and conversion, the unexpected turning around, the shifting to the opposite. Kate Croy says at the end of James's *The Wings of the Dove*: "We shall never be again as we were!" Irreversible reversal is at the core of history and story. "It was not as it had been" (5, 140). "It's not what one would have foretold" (309), says Charles of Sebastian. Reversal is unexpected (178) as well as irreversible.

The fountain, which once was life-giving, quickening, has become dry. The tabernacle lamp, once burning, is extinguished, but then rekindled; the consecrated altar is stripped, but then reconsecrated. (The rekindling and the reconsecration are not mere restorations of what preceded the destruction which was the first reversal.) The altar is in the chapel, which is newest, last built, the latest addition to Brideshead, which had grown over the years and was first built of the stones of another house torn down, the Castle. The Castle (79, 332, 351) is to the New House, Brideshead, as Brideshead is to the chapel (334). But the new style of the chapel is distasteful to Charles.

In the British editions there are chapter headings. "Sebastian contra mundum" occurs twice, the first time when Sebastian turns against his mother's plans to keep him at Oxford; the second time when Cordelia tells of Sebastian turning to the monastery near Carthage.

The reversal of Charles's relation to Catholicism, Charles's conversion, is a reversal from "nonsense," "bosh," "superstition and trickery," "tomfoolery," "witchcraft and hypocrisy," "mumbo-jumbo" (86, 221,

---

8. The 1960 British edition divides into three Books: Book I, Chapters 1–8, becomes I, 1–5, and II, 1–3; Book II becomes III. In the revised edition Book II is called "Brideshead Deserted." The new division emphasizes the movement from charm to death.

9. From "The Queer Feet" in the collection *The Innocence of Father Brown*, by G. K. Chesterton (not *The Wisdom of Father Brown*; see *Brideshead Revisited*, pp. 133, 220). The story tells of the conversion of the thief Flambeau.

The Death of Charm and the Advent of Grace   95

290, 324, 325, 327, 335) to "a prayer, an ancient, newly learned form of words" (350). The images of reversal come to a high point in the epic simile for Charles's conversion: the avalanche (310–11, 341). The thawing sun destroys the little warm and lighted place.

The Greek word for charm and for grace is the same: *charis*. It begins with the letter *chi*, which is written X. The Greek word for anointing begins with the same letter, the word from which our word "*ch*rism," the oil of anointing, and "*Ch*rist," the one anointed, are derived. The letter *chi* also gives us our word "*chi*asm." A chiasm is a mirroring, a reverse imaging. The chiastic structure of *Brideshead Revisited* is displayed in the following diagrams.

The movement from charm to death is the movement from the enclosed and enchanted garden, of which Charles says, "I shall never go back" (31; 169, cf. 299), to the garden of Gethsemane (319). The emblem of this movement is the "skull . . . in a bowl of roses . . . the motto *Et in Arcadia ego* inscribed on its forehead" (42). And the model of this movement is the destruction of the temple in Jerusalem: "How lonely sits the city that was full of people" (*Quomodo sedet sola civitas*), from the lamentation of Jeremiah, is sung at the beginning of the three days of the Holy Week liturgy of death and resurrection, at the Matins for Holy Thursday.[10] The words occur three times in *Brideshead Revisited* (220, 237, 351), and they are crucial to the meaning of the work.

The Crucifixion is the fuller meaning, the deeper sense of, first, the destruction of the temple in Jerusalem; second, the destruction of the houses, Brideshead and Marchmain House; third, the destruction of the body: the death of Lady Marchmain, the death of Julia's baby, the death of Lord Marchmain; and, fourth, the destruction of love and hope: the decline of Sebastian and of Julia (Julia bolts to Rex as Sebastian bolts to drink), and the separation of Charles and Julia: "there was a wall of fire between Julia and me" (337).

When Lord Marchmain makes the sign of the cross after the touch of the chrism, Charles remembers "the veil of the temple being rent from top to bottom" (339).

But the Crucifixion is the beginning of the great reversal, the Resurrection. Out of death and destruction and lamentation come life and restoration and rejoicing. Although the original is irrecoverable, yet there is turning around, reversal and conversion, transforming restoration. Out of emptiness comes a new fullness, which is more than the original, more than the destroyed fullness.

10. Before changes made by Pius XII.

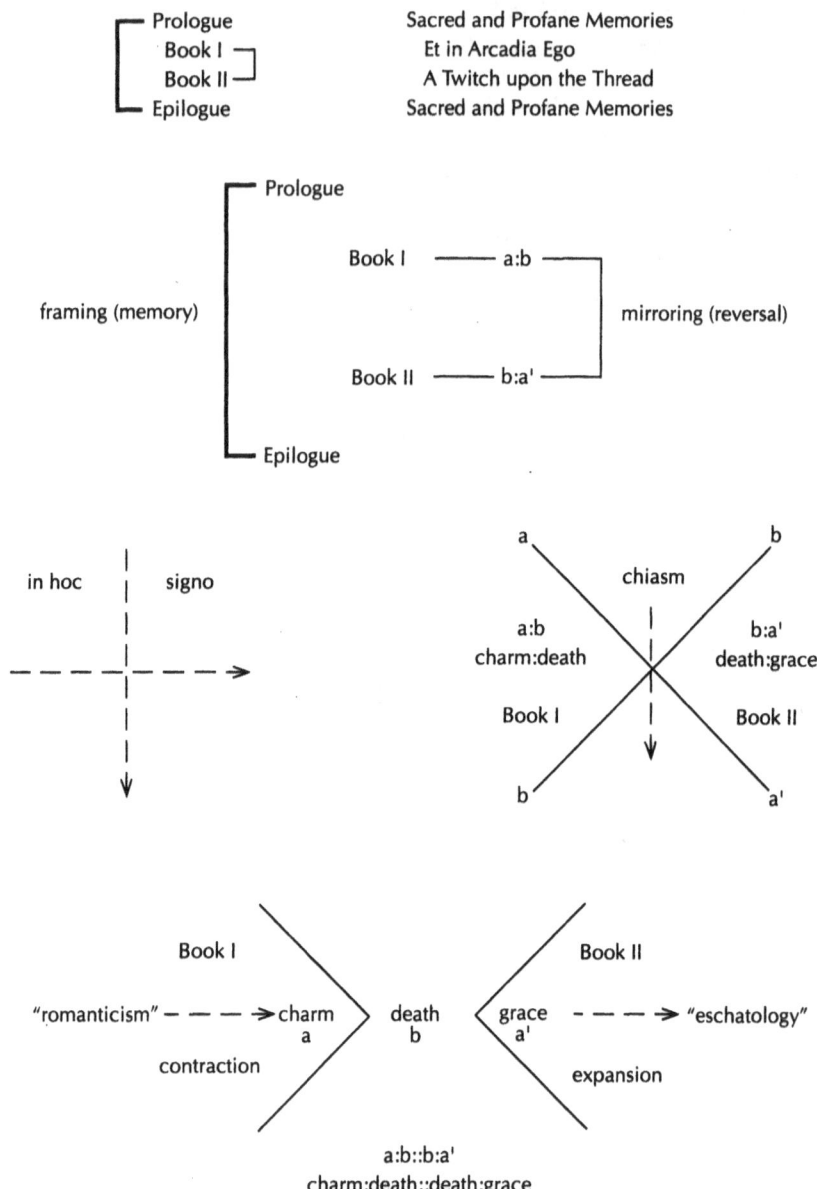

But before the theme of the reversals from life to death to fuller life is developed, something more is to be said of architecture and painting and of the themes of imaging and reversal: architectural painting as combining the themes of imaging and reversal.

The act of building and the buildings themselves have a sense hidden and unexpectedly revealed, says Charles: "The builders did not know the uses to which their work would descend" (350–51); "I became an architectural painter. I have always loved building, holding it to be not only the highest achievement of man but one in which, at the moment of consummation, things were most clearly taken out of his hands and perfected, without his intention, by other means" (226). First there is destruction: "the jungle was creeping back" (227); "It's just another jungle closing in" (232); but then an unexpected purpose, a purpose not intended by the builders, is revealed. The flame is relit before the tabernacle, and the reopened chapel serves the soldiers, of whom Captain Ryder is one: "Something quite remote from anything the builders intended has come out of their work" (351).

Charles's architectural painting is a preserving reversal, a reversal, by means of imaging, of the destroying reversal of the buildings imaged. His painting preserves in an image a beauty that is being destroyed by the jungle closing in. Charles says his work is "to make portraits of houses that were soon to be deserted or debased" (227). His images are works that reverse the destruction of houses, but they are only paintings of houses, not houses; Charles is only a painter, not a builder.

Waugh's work of art, his work as a word-image of ways of life about to be destroyed, is itself imaged within the work by Charles's paintings of buildings ruined or about to be debased or destroyed.

Now we return to the great reversal, the Resurrection following out of the Crucifixion, and to the imaging of that reversal in sacrament.

First, there is the thinness of the signs of grace. Father Mackay says of the anointing, "It is something so small, no show about it" (336). This thinness, this lack of show, is the reverse of that display without which there is no charm. "There was in him no appearance that would attract us to him" (Isaiah 53:2). And of the sign asked for, the sign of conversion, Charles says, "It seemed so small a thing" (338). This is foreshadowed in his first visit to Brideshead: "That is the full account of my first brief visit to Brideshead; could I have known then that so small a thing, in other days, would be remembered with tears by a middle-aged captain of infantry?" (40).

Then there is the reversal from thinness to the fullness of the gift given in the sacrament: "I knew that the sign I had asked for was not a little thing, not a passing nod of recognition" (338); the sign is the sign of the cross, the veil of the temple being rent from top to bottom, the sign of the acceptance of the gift of anointing, the sign of the death out of which comes the gift of the fullness of life. (In the third 1945 British edition: "I prayed more simply; 'God forgive him his sins' and 'Please God, make him accept your forgiveness'" [296].)

This is the importance of the chapel, built by Lord Marchmain as a wedding gift to his wife when she came to Brideshead. The chapel is the last of the building and the newest, and bad art, closed at the death of Lady Marchmain, but opened and used again in the Age of Hooper for the memorial presencing, the representation of the great reversal from the death of Crucifixion to the abundant life of Resurrection, the chapel used for the sacrament of the altar, the sacrament signed by the flame of the lamp relit. In the last pages of the book, at the end of the Epilogue, Charles, having turned back toward his past, remembering the past out of which came his turning around, his conversion, visits the chapel and turns forward: "You're looking unusually cheerful today" are the last words of the work.

Whose story is the story of *Brideshead Revisited*? It is the story of all who undergo reversal, conversion, by the intertwining of their lives: "the fate of more souls than one was at issue" (326). The story is told by a colorless teller; the course of events is narrated or represented as seen through the transparent eye of Charles's memory. Charles is the narrating center looking back toward the conversions in "the household of the faith,"[11] toward Sebastian's conversion, Lord Marchmain's conversion, Julia's conversion. Thus Charles's own conversion is presented with exquisite indirection; it is told only on the edge of the telling of the other conversions which bring it about. It is seen only on the edge of the field of vision, the center of which is filled by the Flyte family.

In relation to the question "whose story is it?" three kinds of characters can be distinguished: first, characters who mirror each other, that is, characters who are reverse images of each other; second, characters who do not undergo reversal, but who enable us to understand and to measure those who do; this kind of character is chorus or foil; third, the character of the narrator of the story, the eye which sees, the present which remembers.

11. Subtitle of the work in an early draft; see *The Letters of Evelyn Waugh*, ed. Mark Amory (New Haven: Ticknor and Fields, 1980), p. 189; also pp. 185, 196, 439. In manuscript the epigraph to the Prologue reads *Non hinc* [sic] *habemus manentem civitatem*. Hebrews 13: 14 reads in the Vulgate *Non enim habemus hic manentem civitatem*. In manuscript under "A Household of Faith" Waugh writes "A Theological Novel."

Characters of the first kind fall into several groups: first, Sebastian and his Teddy-bear, and Lady Marchmain and her little talks mirror each other. The charm of helpless childhood and the power of charm to control, the evasion of responsibility for oneself and the oppressive providence of taking too much responsibility for others (215) are reverse images of each other. Second, Rex's conversion is the comically reversed image of Charles's conversion. Third, the exposure of illusion without substance in Samgrass and Rex ("Samgrass revealed" and "Rex revealed" are chapter headings) is the reverse image of charm as the forerunner of grace. Charm is not illusion without substance, but forerunner. Sebastian is the forerunner of Julia (75–76, 178–79, 257, 303). Lord Marchmain is the forerunner of Sebastian (98): "You see, *it's all happened before*" (136); "You see, I've been through all this before" (163). Julia says, "Perhaps I'm only a forerunner, too"; and Charles: "Perhaps all our loves are . . . types," that is, forerunners (303; cf. 79). The third 1945 British edition reads "vagabond-language scrawled on gateposts and paving stones along the weary road" (265). This is the place of the intertwining of beauty and sadness in Julia (239–40, 310), like death in Arcady.

Characters of the second kind (those who do not undergo reversal) are, first, Anthony Blanche and Cara, figures on the edge of the action who comment on and explain the action. Both are sexually and socially marginal, and both take us closer to the center of the truth. During the dinner at Thame, Anthony warns against charm (50–57), with a reprise in the bar after the exhibition of the Latin American paintings (270–73). In Venice Cara says of Sebastian that he is "in love with his own childhood" (the letter from Sebastian: "I am mourning for my lost innocence" [72]), and she says of Lord Marchmain: "I protect him from his own innocence" (102–3). Together Anthony and Cara foreshadow for us that charm and innocence are marked for death. Second, there are also those who stake out by their steady character the framework that enables us to measure the reversals undergone by others, those like Fortinbras, "Strong-in-Arm," in *Hamlet*. Measuring, in their different ways, as a kind of rule of faith, the reversals from charm to death and from death to grace, are Nanny Hawkins, withdrawn; Cordelia, plain; Bridey, dull and tactless; and the priests, Father Phipps, Father Mowbray, Father Mackay, colorless, transparent, thin sacramental signs.

Third, there is the character of Charles. Nancy Mitford calls him "dim";[12] he is the colorless eye, the eye which must lack color in order

---

12. *Letters*, p. 196.

to see all colors. *Brideshead Revisited* belongs to the genre of the *Bildungsroman*, the account of the passage from innocence to experience, and Charles's innocence is presented as colorless.

Charles needs the Flyte family from which to draw life. Without them he is unformed, pale, empty, "dim." What color and fullness his life has are parasitic on the Flyte family. Through his involvement with that household of the faith he, drawn by charm as forerunner, comes to grace; he is converted, but that conversion does not make up for the loss of the natural life he loses when he loses first Sebastian and then Julia. The death of his hope of living at Brideshead as the husband of Julia (321–22, 327–28) leaves him naturally empty. For artistic reasons Waugh makes Charles dim because Charles is the colorless eye which sees all colors; but for theological reasons Waugh makes Charles dim because the gain of the life of grace does not substitute for nature in nature's own terms and on nature's own terms. "Happiness doesn't seem to have much to do with it" (89). "Can't they even let him die in peace?" "They mean something so different by 'peace'" (324; cf. 279). Of Julia it is said: "Her religion stood as a barrier between her and her natural goal" (181; cf. 291, 340). "It seems to me that without your religion Sebastian would have the chance to be a happy and healthy man" (145; cf. 163).

The limits that the acceptance of grace can set to the demand for natural happiness and peace and the limits that Waugh the artist has set to the availability for the reader of the inwardness of Charles's conversion are both brought under the thinness of the sacramental sign: what the sacrament in its fullness is is incommensurate with what it looks to be, although what the sacrament is is not separable from what it looks to be. Sacramentality is between sentimentality, lack of distance, on the one hand, and satire, emphatic distance, on the other hand.

Brideshead, Sebastian and Julia—the forerunners—are later seen to have been more than they had seemed to be, but they could not have been instruments of providence ("part of a plan," 259–60; cf. 183) without also being what they seemed to be: charm and love, gracing with the grace of nature.

The sacred and the profane memories of Captain Charles Ryder are neither separated from each other nor merged into indiscrete indistinctness; rather they are intertwined, like the members of a household or the partners of a partnership.

On the dust jacket of the 1945 British edition there is a "Warning" by Waugh:

> When I wrote my first novel sixteen years ago, my publishers advised me, and I readily agreed, to prefix the warning that it was "meant to be funny."

The phrase proved a welcome gift to unsympathetic critics. Now, in a more sombre decade, I must provide them with another text, and, in honesty to the patrons who have supported me hitherto, state that *Brideshead Revisited* is *not* meant to be funny. There are passages of buffoonery, but the general theme is at once romantic and eschatological.

It is ambitious, perhaps intolerably presumptuous; nothing less than an attempt to trace the workings of the divine purpose in a pagan world, in the lives of an English Catholic family, half-paganized themselves, in the world of 1923–1939. The story will be uncongenial alike to those who look back on that pagan world with unalloyed affection, and to those who see it as transitory, insignificant and, already, hopefully passed. Whom then can I hope to please? Perhaps those who have the leisure to read a book word by word for the interest of the writer's use of language; perhaps those who look to the future with black forebodings and need more solid comfort than rosy memories. For the latter I have given my hero, and them, if they will allow me, a hope, not indeed, that anything but disaster lies ahead, but that the human spirit, redeemed, can survive all disasters.

Brideshead Revisited: Brideshead is, first, the color seen through the colorless eye; second, the charm which is the forerunner of grace; and third, the household of the faith which leads Charles to faith. But the loss of Brideshead and the Flyte family leaves Charles empty: "homeless, childless, middle-aged, loveless" (350). Nevertheless—and this is the reversal, the conversion, which means that Charles will never again be as he was before—through his turn to faith, in spite of the emptiness in which he is left by the loss of Brideshead, Charles lives a new life with the pledge and hope of glory, a beauty beyond both charm and death, a life signed and given, but not in natural fruition and fulfillment, which, taken as idol or rival and not as icon or forerunner, is "such a prospect perhaps as a high pinnacle of the temple afforded after the hungry days in the desert and the jackal-haunted nights" (322). Charles leads a new life signed and given in the gracious sacrament of the altar, in which he rejoices. "Vanity of vanities, all is vanity . . . is not the last word" (351).

Arthur Evelyn St. John Waugh made a formal and solemn entry in his diary on 24 June 1944: *Brideshead Revisited* was completed on the Feast of Corpus Christi. In a letter of 30 March 1966, he wrote, "I now cling to the Faith doggedly without joy."[13] Eleven days later he died at his home, Combe Florey House, after Mass on Easter Sunday.

---

13. *The Diaries of Evelyn Waugh*, ed. Michael Davie (Boston: Little, Brown and Company, 1976), p. 568. *Letters*, p. 639.

On the last page of the proofs corrected in November 1944 in Croatia, Waugh deleted, after "said the second-in-command," these last words: "'have you had a good morning?' 'Yes, thank you,' I said; 'a very good morning.'" He also deleted the words

ADDENDA ON IMITATION

John Plant says, in the first edition (1942) of *Work Suspended*, "the girders and struts" of what is represented are both adorned and concealed by the style of representation, by "false domes, superfluous columns" and by "plaster and gilt" (p. 2). The fourth British edition (1946) of *Brideshead Revisited* reads "The dome was false..." (p. 33; p. 44 in the 1960 edition). See Robert Murray Davis, "Textual Problems in the Novels of Evelyn Waugh," *Papers of the Bibliographical Society of America* 62 (1968), pp. 261–62.

In the interview given to Julian Jebb in *Paris Review* 30 (1963), Waugh says, "All fictional characters are flat. A writer can give an illusion of depth by giving an apparently steroscopic view of a character—seeing him from two vantage points;..." (p. 110). See the paragraph on "the use of live men in books" in the first edition (1942) of *Work Suspended*, pp. 82–83.

ADDENDA ON STRUCTURE

"It is time to speak of Julia..." (178) is at the center; it is the beginning of the seventh of thirteen chapters; it is preceded and followed by an almost equal number of pages. At the center is the turn from Sebastian to Julia.

Just as Sebastian is the forerunner of Julia, so Book I ends with Charles seeing Sebastian for the last time and with the "afflatus" (225) or "inspiration" (227) of artistic power: "There were no difficulties..." (218); and Book II ends with Charles parting from Julia and with the advent of faith: "I do understand" (341). "I had felt the brush take life in my hand..." (222; cf. 82) is the forerunner of "The avalanche was down..." (341).

"... [T]his little cloud, the size of a man's hand, that was going to swell into a storm among us" (324) is an allusion to I Kings 18: 44, interpreted in the Carmelite tradition as a "type" of the *Theotokos*.

---

shown in brackets: "... the flame which the old knights saw from their tombs, which they saw put out, [while the waggons rolled past, carting away the walls of their stronghold, and the black gowned Hoopers rustled and croaked above their bones;] that flame burns again for other soldiers, far from home, farther, in heart, than Acre or Jerusalem, [heavier in heart than the toiling waggons.] ... burning anew among the old stones." The Castle is to Brideshead as Brideshead is to the chapel, but the flame in the chapel is the same as the flame in the Castle. See *Later Writings of Bishop Hooper,* "edited for the Parker Society for the Publication of the Works of the Fathers and Early Writers of the Reformed English Church," vol. 21 (Cambridge: Cambridge University Press, 1852), pp. 401ff.: "Res controversa inter nos catholicos et Neotericos Romanos de eucharistia tribus constat capitibus"—"The issue between us catholics and the Innovating Romans concerning the Eucharist falls under three headings."

Scholium I (Chapter 11)
Two Doxologies: Argument and Praise

The philosopher, like everyone else, has always already accepted or taken as granted a *doxa* (1005b33) which is first and last (*ibid.*) presuppositionless and unsubordinated (1005b14, 16). But, unlike everyone else, the philosopher has eros for giving a justification or an account (*logon didonai*), even (or especially) an account of the first and last, the presuppositionless and unsubordinated *doxa*.

As philosopher Aristotle needs the un-naturalness of a freak or monster, the opponent who opposes in speech the differences (among kinds, *sēmainein ti*, 1006a21, and between truth and falsity) without which there is no *logos*. But this un-naturalness is subordinate to nature: being as *eidos*, *horos* (boundary, term, demarcation, definition), *logos*, and *nous*-ing the first and last *doxa*. It is only by displaying in speech the self-refutation in speech of such an opponent that the philosopher achieves a *logos* (cf. 1142a25–26, 1143a36–b2) of the *nous*-ed *doxa*.[1] It is only by thus using the freakish and monstrous unnaturalness of the opponent that the philosopher achieves the acme of (his) nature.

Nietzsche[2] says that creativity has primacy, and he reduces nature to the unarticulated and the indeterminate (*to aoriston*, 1007b27–29; *a-horos*) in order to confront creativity with the least resistance from whatever it faces over against itself.[3]

---

1. Does rest (*nous, intellectus, intuitus*) include a potentiality for being complemented by motion (*logos, ratio, discursus*)?

2. Nietzsche, *Sämtliche Werke*, ed. G. Colli and M. Montinari, Kritische Studienausgabe (Berlin and New York: de Gruyter; Munich: Deutscher Taschenbuch Verlag, 1980), vols. 12, 13: 2(108, 119, 174), 6(23), 9(41, 48, 60, 79, 89, 91, 97, 106, 136, 144), 10(19, 145, 154, 159), 11(87, 415).

3. Nietzsche sometimes says that the greater the resistance overcome and mastered, the greater the exhilaration in overcoming and mastering. See, for example, 14(174).

The unity of Nietzsche's "will to power" (foreshadowed by "critical history") and "eternal return of the same" (foreshadowed by "monumental history") can be read against the background of Aristotle, *On Interpretation* IX: the future insofar as it is yet to come about by choice is indeterminate, but once it has come about (*fieri: factum est*)

For Aquinas creativity is one "side" of the eternity and the necessity, the self-sufficiency, of God: creativity is the "back side" of the primary sense of nature (God), the "side" which faces what is other than God if God freely chooses that there be beings (created natures) other than God (God could have chosen that there be no beings other than His self-sufficient being, His nature). Creatures praise the goodness of God (this praise is called "doxology") as being such that it would not be less good if there were no creatures.[4]

Aristotle and Aquinas include the un-naturalness and the creativity which are self-destructively praised by Nietzsche, but they include these within the primacy of nature.

---

as a determinate chosen present, the truth that it has indeed so come about is perpetual (eternal after-the-fact) and unalterable (necessary after-the-fact). This quasi-eternal-and-necessary having-been-chosen past, as exemplary for new choices and as imitated by new choices, determines as an already-chosen choice what would otherwise be the indeterminate future, the open future yet to be determined by a not-yet-chosen choice. ("Monumental history" and "critical history": see the second essay of *Thoughts out of Season*, "The Advantage and Disadvantage of Information about the Past (*Historie*) for Living.")

Nietzschean "courage" in relation to contingency (being able to be otherwise) and community (being with others): *Thoughts Out of Season* IV 3 *in fine*.

4. Preface to the Canon of the Mass, Weekdays IV:

   ... we do well always and everywhere to give you thanks.
   You have no need of our praise,
   yet our desire to thank you is itself your gift.
   Our prayer of thanksgiving adds nothing to your greatness,
   but makes us grow in your grace. ...

Aquinas, *Quaestio disputata de potentia Dei* IV 2, ad 5: "... non in ipsis rebus conditis quasi in fine quievit, sed a rebus conditis in se ipso, in quo sua beatitudo consistit, permansit (cum non sit beatus ex eo quod res fecerit, sed ex hoc quod in se ipso sufficientiam habens rebus factis non indiget)..." [... God did not rest in created things themselves as if in an end, but He rested from created things, remaining in Himself, in whom His blessédness consists, because He is not blesséd in this that He created things, but in this that having sufficiency in Himself He does not need created things . . .].

Scholium II   (Chapter 12)
Glosses on Heidegger's Architectonic Word-Play

I

This title promises a gloss on Heidegger's words, more exactly, on four of his words, four words that are crucial to his thought after *Sein und Zeit*. These four words fall into two groups of two:

Lichtung and *Ereignis*
and
Bergung and *Wahrnis*.

The promise of a gloss on these words is formulated as a provocative oxymoron, spanned between architectonic and play. Kant tells us in *The Critique of Pure Reason* (B86off.) that "architectonic" means "the unity of a manifold ... under one idea, ... a common root": "the affinity of parts is from a single end which makes the parts into a whole." The parts, because of their relation to the end, are related one to another with necessity. Aristotle in the *Poetics* (1451a30ff.) speaks of a necessity of the whole so stringent that nothing can be added and nothing can be taken away. This necessity is called organic because the parts are related as the parts of an animal are related one to another: all the parts together as a whole are ordered toward and by the to-be-achieved achievements of the animal (*telos, energeiai*). Contrasted with this systematic necessity is what Aristotle calls *sōros* (1040b8–9, 1041b11–12, 1044a4–5, 1045a8–14), a heap, and what Kant calls a mere aggregate or rhapsody, a being together which is open to arbitrary addition and subtraction.

In speaking of Heidegger's word-play do we mean a lack of such unity of end and necessity of relation, something jerry-built, thrown together at random out of bits and pieces found lying around, a kind of punning, like "bark" having to do with dogs and trees and water, in contrast to "healthy," analyzed by Aristotle (1060b31ff.) as a cluster of irreducibly different meanings nevertheless oriented toward one end (*pros hen*), irreducibly different meanings organized in terms of that one last end?

If we can speak at all of Heidegger's word-play as organized toward such a privileged one, that one is certainly not something exhaustively present, nor is it exhaustive presence itself (*nous*), presence as distinguished from that-which-is-present, and it is not something absent either, not even absence itself—nor is it the interplay of presence and absence: presence/absence (*Sein*).

Is there then an architectonic of these four crucial words, and if not, are we left with the alternative, a jumble, at best a rhapsody, the pastime of a child or a madman playing with fragments of the tradition, heaping them together and smashing them apart at will?

II

Heidegger's use of the four crucial words is shot through with reversal and ambivalence and with the troping or twisting of a usual and ordinary meaning toward the unusual and extraordinary, which nevertheless keeps its roots in the matrix of the usual and ordinary.

The verb *lichten* in ordinary usage has to do with clearing off land and with lifting anchor. The noun *Lichtung* means light in the sense of free of, not closed off or held down, not heavy, as in "light as a feather," unencumbered by and thus open for. *Lichtung* is the forest clearing in which is cleared away whatever would occlude light from making visible what is there in the clearing to be seen. Thus early on (*Sein und Zeit*, 14. Aufl., 133 and note a; 350–51) Heidegger associates *Lichtung* with light in the sense of brightness (*Licht, Helle*). But later there is a reversal, an emphatic disassociation of *Lichtung* from light in the sense of brightness and bringing to light, and a focus on the sense of not held down by or bound to or filled up with: *das Freie, das Offene*: the free and open.

The ordinary sense of *Ereignis* is event. Heidegger shifts from this usual meaning toward two other meanings. The first shift or trope returns to the root of the word *Ereignis: Auge:* eye. *Ereignis* is indeed derived from *Er-äug-nis*, be-eye-ing, although today no German ear hears that root in the word; the relation to *Auge*, eye, is a sunken etymology. But Heidegger charges the word *Ereignis* with another, second unusual meaning, hearing in the word, against all etymology, the root *eigen*, own, so that the meaning different from the ordinary meaning, event, is ambivalent: the extraordinary meaning is not only

Scholium II   107

eyeing but also owning. Heidegger approves *appropriement* (*Gesamtausgabe*, vol. 15, 365; vol. 65, 320, 489) as the French translation of *Ereignis*: appropriation, coming into its own or taking to itself as its own.

Both *bergen* and *wahren* (*bewahren*, *verwahren*) have the sense of save or protect. Jetsam from a shipwreck can be salvaged, *geborgen*. The place where luggage is left safely for a time in a railway station is the *Gepäckaufbewahrung*. To hold out against opposition, preserving one's own, is *sich gegen etwas verwahren*.

But because *bergen* also means to hide (*verbergen*), to undo this hiding (*entbergen*) is to disclose, to display, to bring to light, to manifest. Manifestness is un-hidden-ness, Greek: *a-lēthe-ia*, truthing as the undoing of *lēthē*, hiddenness. And the ordinary word for true is *wahr* and for truth *Wahrheit*.

Here we come up against another ambiguity. *Wahr(nis)* means *both* undoing hiddenness by manifesting, truth as display, *and* hiding or protecting against this undoing, protecting against this manifesting. And thirdly *Wahrnis* also means protection against the very interplay hiddenness/manifestness itself, protection against both poles of the interplay in their interrelatedness (*Gegenwendigkeit*). In this last sense *Wahrnis* means a coming into its own (*Ereignis*), free from and clear of (*Lichtung*) being bound into the interplay hiddenness (*Verbergung*)/manifestness (*Entbergung*).

$Truth_1$ is manifestation out of hiddenness, the undoing of hiddenness, un-hiddenness, display; $truth_2$ is hiddenness as protection ($Wahrnis_1$) against being assaulted by the demand for exhaustive manifestation out of hiddenness; $truth_3$ is withdrawnness from and protection ($Wahrnis_2$) against the hiddenness/manifestness interplay, whether the accent within that interplay fall on manifestation ($truth_1$) out of hiddenness or on hiddenness as protection ($truth_2$) against being assaulted by excessive demand for manifestation out of hiddenness:

$truth_1$ $Wahrheit_1$
$truth_2$ $Wahrheit_2$ $Wahrnis_1$ $Un\text{-}Wahrheit_1$ un-$truth_1$ not $truth_1$
$truth_3$ $Wahrnis_2$ $Un\text{-}Wahrheit_2$ un-$truth_2$ not $truth_2$

Thus the four crucial words in the crisscrossing and the twisting and turning of their meanings, in the reversals, ambivalences, and tropings, are an architectonic play, a playful architectonic, organized, it is true, toward one end, but toward an end neither present nor absent, an end not even presence/absence and manifestness/hiddenness themselves.

III

1. *Lichtung* ("clearing [away], lightening [up], opening [up]" as other than "shining, brightening") and *Ereignis* ("appropriation: clearing away the inappropriate, coming into its own; taking as its own" as other than "eyeing") are protection (*Bergung, Wahrnis*), protection against reduction to the interplay hiddenness/manifestness. That interplay, hiddenness/manifestness, is not the last space; that interplay takes place and is played out in the space called *Lichtung*, a space which comes into its own (*sich ereignet*) as other than the interplay hiddenness/manifestness.

2. *Lichtung* and *Ereignis* fall into hiddenness/manifestness. In this fall *Lichtung* becomes brightness (*Licht, Helle*), and *Ereignis* becomes eyeing (*Eräugnis*). (This fall is from beyond the interplay into one partner of the interplay: manifestness: brightness for eyeing.) *Bergung* comes into the interplay *Verbergung/Entbergung* and *Verborgenheit/Unverborgenheit*, and *Wahrnis* comes into the interplay *Unwahrheit/Wahrheit$_1$*. (This fall is from beyond the interplay into the other partner of the interplay: hiddenness: withdrawnness from view.)

3. Hiddenness (*Verbergung, Verborgenheit; Un-Wahrheit$_1$ = Wahrheit$_2$*) is protection against another reduction, reduction to manifestation understood as attack on hiddenness, war waged against hiddenness, wresting hiddenness into manifestness, rather than letting manifestness rest in an excess of hiddenness. Hiddenness is thus *Bergung* and *Wahrnis* as protection against excessive demand for manifestness, protection against reduction to availability for representation (*Vorstellung, Gegenständlichkeit*) and protection against reduction to availability for manipulation (*Ge-stell, Bestellbarkeit, Bestand*).

4. Manifestation is the process of manifesting out of hiddenness. Manifestation is translation of hiddenness into manifestness *of* that-which-*is*(-manifest). Because manifesting the manifestation of that-which-*is*(-manifest) turns manifestation itself into a that-which-*is*(-manifest), manifestation out of hiddenness falls into that-which-is. But looking among the characteristics of beings for what-it-means-to-be, we discover—nothing, no-thing, no that-which-is. Looking at that-which-*is*(-manifest), we forget manifestness itself.

5. Because that-which-is is both hidden and manifest, there can be false *doxa* (view: both the show itself and how we take the show, what we take the show *as* being). False *doxa* comes about when that-which-is both shows itself ("is manifest") and, because it is also being beyond the show ("is hidden"), is taken *as* being other than it *is*. The difference between show and *as* is formulated when we say something *of* some-

thing. When there is one show (snub-nose) and two *as* (both Theaetetus and Socrates), then error is possible: we take the shown snub-nosed one we see *as* being Socrates, but he *is* Theaetetus. We say falsely, "The snub-nosed one is Socrates." When there is one show and two *as*, two (both Theaetetus and Socrates) having the same show (snub-nose) in common, we can take the common show *as* being the show of the other (Socrates) rather than of the one (Theaetetus): we twist and falsely say something *of* something. Hidden/manifest is thus reduced to saying incorrectly and, set against and contrasted with this incorrectness, to saying correctly: true assertion is assertion not twisted but in line with that-which-is: true assertion corresponds to that-which-is.

6. The fall$_1$ into the interplay hiddenness/manifestness; the fall$_2$ of hiddenness into manifestation; the fall$_3$ of manifestation into that-which-*is*(-manifest); the fall$_4$ of the hidden/manifest into the incorrectly/correctly said—all these falls are not mistakes to be corrected; rather they are to be let take place, to be let to come into their own out of *Lichtung* and *Ereignis*, out of in the twofold sense of away from and owed to. What comes out of and thus turns away from somehow still remains in what it is owed to.

7. Manipulation and representation of that-which-*is*(-hidden/manifest) and the interplay hiddenness/manifestation itself can turn around out of their fall, turn back toward letting come into its own (*Ereignis*) what they are always still owed to: the clearing (*Lichtung*) or space in which the interplay hiddenness/manifestness is let take place as protected against remaining fallen into that-which-*is*(-hidden/manifest) as represented and manipulated.[1]

1. Some references:
A. *Lichtung: Gesamtausgabe (GA)* (Frankfurt am Main: Klostermann, 1975ff.) vol. 15, 262; cf. vol. 34, 59; *Zur Sache des Denkens (SD)* (Tübingen: Niemeyer, 1969), 72; *Zur Frage nach der Bestimmung der Sache des Denkens (FBSD)* (St. Gallen: Erker, 1984), 17; *Zollikoner Seminare (ZSem)* (Frankfurt am Main: Klostermann, 1987), 16.

B. *Anwesen/Anwesendes; Sein/Seiendes: Sein und Zeit (SZ)*, 14. Aufl. (Tübingen: Niemeyer, 1977), 6; *GA* vol. 9, 478–79; vol. 26, 195, 252; vol. 29/30, 405; vol. 54, 223; *ZSem*, 229.

C. *nous:* SZ, 33; GA vol. 31, 73–109.

D. Plato, *Theaetetus: GA* vol. 34, 285–322.

E. *SZ*, 36–37; *GA* vol. 5, 264–65; vol. 9, 332–33, 441–43; vol. 12, 246–49, 253, note b; vol. 15, 373, 403–7, 438; vol. 34, 142–43; vol. 63, 76; vol. 65, 381; *SD*, 20–23, 58, 78–80; *FBSD*, 19; *ZSem*, 216; *Vorträge und Aufsätze* (Pfullingen: Neske, 1954), 135, 276–79; *Was heißt Denken?* (Tübingen: Niemeyer, 1954), 97; *Identität und Differenz* (Pfullingen: Neske, 1957), 24–25; *Nietzsche*, Bd. 2 (Pfullingen: Neske, 1961), 378; *Die Technik und die Kehre* (Pfullingen: Neske, 1962), 41–45; *Denkerfahrungen* (Frankfurt am Main: Klostermann, 1983), 147–49, 175–79; *Von der Un-Verborgenheit: Fridolin Wiplingers Bericht von einem Gespräch mit Martin Heidegger*, aufgezeichnet von E. Fräntski (Pfaffenweiler: Centaurus-Verlagsgesellschaft, 1987), 8, 14, 20, 21–22, 23, 31–42 (esp. 34–36, 41–42), 46–47, 52–56 (esp. 56), 58.

Scholium III (Chapter 12)
Heidegger between (Gadamer's) Plato and Aristotle

Gadamer's reading of the first non-fragmentary and non-quoted philosophical texts available to us, the Platonic dialogues,[1] especially of *Sophist* and *Philebus*, calls into question Heidegger's reading of Greek philosophy as a falling off from a beginning caught up in the interplay (*Gegenwendigkeit*) of hiddenness and display (*alētheia*), a falling off through Plato toward Aristotle's apotheosis, in *Metaphysics* IX, 10 and XII, 7 and 9, of presence without absence: for Aristotle the primary sense of *ousia* is *nous* without the otherness (*krinein*) and the motion (*kinein*) of *logos*. For Gadamer the root of the Platonic dialogue form is the Indeterminate Two of Plato's unwritten teaching. The dialogue form displays (*in actu exercito*) the protectedness (*Bergung*) of the open-ended and intrinsically never-ending interplay of speakers and of speeches, a protectedness Plato is said to have called the Indeterminate Two, the wedge of doubleness inexorably splitting and delaying presence and display. Protecting absence and hiddenness from being swallowed up in presence and display, the Indeterminate Two protects the *lēthē* in *alētheia* and thus prevents philosophy from degenerating into doctrine and pursuit of the honoring of doctrine. Gadamer reads Plato by using Heidegger's *Bergung* against Heidegger's reading of Plato. He lets us see Heidegger's *Bergung* in the context of (Gadamer's) Plato and of Aristotle, Aristotle's apotheosis of presence and display without absence and hiddenness: Aristotle's *ousia* as *nous* without the otherness and the motion of *logos*, mind without the form of dialogue.

The One and the Indeterminate Two of (Gadamer's) Plato let (or lets) come about a *not* (not_1) different from the *not* (not_2) of *eidē* to one another; not_2 is the *not* of otherness of *eidē* to one another: $eidos_a$ is merely other than $eidos_b$; $eidos_x$ and $eidos_y$ exclude each other. Not_2 lets

---

1. See Chapter 12, note 1.

a being display itself or be viewed as another what (*eidos*), as *another what* which it nevertheless *is*, or as a what (*eidos*) *other* than any what which it *is* (or which it could be), as a what which it is *not*. a/b: a human$_a$ being (Theaetetus) sits$_a$ [said while Theaetetus sits]; x/y: a human$_x$ being (Theaetetus) stands$_y$ [said while Theaetetus sits] or a human$_x$ being (Theaetetus) flies$_y$.

Not$_1$ lets a different doubleness of *Sein/Schein* come about, a doubleness which is simpler and more widespread than those othernesses which *not*$_2$ lets come about: the othernesses *eidos*$_a$/*eidos*$_b$ and *eidos*$_x$/*eidos*$_y$. This different doubleness of *Sein/Schein* is to be (*Sein*) "is/is not" display (*Schein*); display is out of hiddenness: display is not hiddenness but not without hiddenness: one (hiddenness) and another one (display) both together are one two: to be:

to be
hiddenness/display.

To be is one two: to be is the hendiadys *alētheia*: hiddenness/display.[2]

From the doubleness of *Sein/Schein* as *esse/lucere* (*sich darstellen*) comes about the doubleness of *Sein/Schein* as *esse/videri* (*sich verstellen*). Here is the place of both the sophist and the politician (*dēmologikos*), the two together, in difference to the philosopher. The sophist and the politician both prefer honor to inquiry (*plus videri quam esse*): they speak in order to be honored.[3]

In Book XII, 7 and 9, of Aristotle's *Metaphysics* (see also Book IX, 10) the primary sense of *ousia*, *noēsis noēseōs*, is display without doubleness: *alētheia* without *lēthē*; presence without the double difference: without absence and without that-which-is-present/absent;[4] *nous* without *kinēsis* and without *logos*, *nous* without *psychē*; *energeia* without *dynamis*; *eidos* without other *eidē* (being without being with others,

---

2. *Reductio ad absurdum*: "To be is display; to be is hiddenness; display is not hiddenness; hiddenness is not display: therefore to be is not to be; if display is and if display is not hiddenness, then hiddenness is not; if hiddenness is and if hiddenness is not display, then display is not."

Conclusion of the *reductio ad absurdum*: to be is *both* hiddenness *and* display; to be is the hendiadys *alētheia*. Heidegger is a (Gadamerian) Platonist, but not a Heideggerian "Platonist." Q.E.D.

3. There is a twisting (*ver-stellen*; "twist": *Zwist, zwei*), twisting$_1$, other than the twisting, twisting$_2$, in which error fails truth (see Scholium II, Part III, Section 5). In twisting$_1$ something true *discovered* through inquiry, something evidenced, is spoken by a speaker who wants to be *honored* for making public the discovered truth—and a philosopher can err (twisting$_2$) even though he lives in inquiry for its own sake and not in order to be honored.

4. Ein "da," das nicht das "da" von etwas ist; ein "da" ohne etwas, das da ist. See *Gesammelte Werke* V, p. 293.

without honor and friendship) and without *genos* (being without having a common background, a background shared with others).[5]

For Heidegger this *ousia-nous* is the apotheosis of what he calls "metaphysics." Heidegger takes a step back behind what he calls "metaphysics," a step toward *Bergung*; this step back is both a step back behind Heidegger's "Plato," a "Plato" without *Bergung*, a Plato stylized by Heidegger into the forerunner of Aristotle's *ousia-nous*, and a step around (Gadamer's) Plato, the Plato of the One and the Indeterminate Two: *Bergung*.

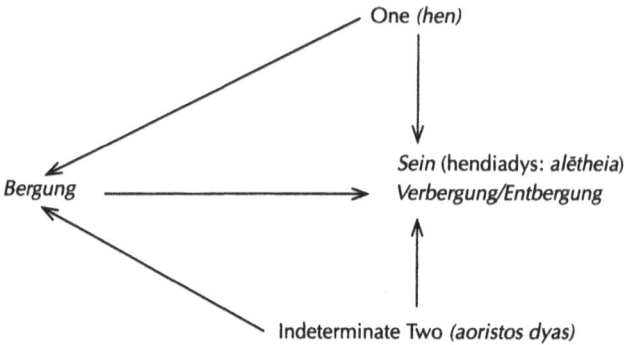

Just as *Bergung* is not *Verbergung/Entbergung* (*alētheia*), so the One/the Indeterminate Two "are" (or "is") not the one number two (hendiadys): the "eidetic number" two: *Sein*.

5. Why does Gadamer insist on infecting the *nous* (*noēsis noēseōs*) of Book XII, 7 and 9, with *kinēsis* and with *logos*, with *psychē* (Aristotle understands soul in terms of movement, *kinein*, and discrimination, *krinein*)? Of course "first for us" *energeia* is embedded in *dynamis*, "first for us" *alētheia* is embedded in *ti kata tinos*, "first for us" *zōē* is embedded in *psychē*, but Aristotle intends to free *nous* as *energeia*, *alētheia*, *zōē* from these embeddednesses. That Aristotle does not succeed in doing what he intends to do is owed, for the Platonist Gadamer, to the power of the Indeterminate Two. See *Gesammelte Werke* III, pp. 11, 295, 403–4; VI, p. 170.

www.ingramcontent.com/pod-product-compliance
Lightning Source LLC
Chambersburg PA
CBHW031423290426
44110CB00011B/503